MW00588563

THE
LITTLE
HISTORY
OF
CORNWALL

THE
LITTLE
HISTORY
OF
CORNWALL

PAUL
WREYFORD

The
History
Press

This book is dedicated to my best friend Douglas Goddard

First published 2018

The History Press
The Mill, Brimscombe Port
Stroud, Gloucestershire, GL5 2QG
www.thehistorypress.co.uk

British Library Cataloguing in Publication Data.
A catalogue record for this book is available from the British Library.

ISBN 978 0 7509 8443 0

Typesetting and origination by The History Press
Printed in Great Britain

CONTENTS

ABOUT THE AUTHOR

Paul Wreyford is a journalist who has worked in the industry for more than twenty-five years, as a reporter, sub-editor and editor on a variety of newspapers and magazines, both in Britain and abroad. He is the author of six local history books, four of which have been published by The History Press.

Although his work has taken him all over the country, Paul considers the West Country to be home.

INTRODUCTION

Some history books are dull; I love history, but even I struggle to get past the first chapter of some of them.

In my opinion, too much detail is sometimes the problem. A scholar of history might want to know everything – but does the average person?

There are plenty of history books on Cornwall and, yes, most are far weightier than this one. However, a clue to the appeal of this book, as far as I am concerned, is in the title. Cornwall might be deserving of a 'big' history book, but the fact that this is a 'little' one actually makes it more accessible to those who would like to know *something*, rather than *everything*.

All the significant events are included in this book, but, due to its size, I have had less opportunity of falling into the trap of providing *too much* detail.

There is no other county in England quite like Cornwall; it is a land apart. Even today access into the duchy is restricted by the River Tamar – its natural border – with only a few crossing places. It is as if those roads into the county are threads that keep Cornwall hanging on to the rest of England, or, more accurately, keep the rest of England hanging on to the still fiercely independent Cornish! There is no doubt that the isolation of Cornwall has shaped the people – and therefore its history – into something quite different from the rest of the country.

I believe most people are curious and would like to know more about the history of their county. Many do not seek to do so because they find some history books daunting. I hope this 'little' book is different.

Paul Wreyford

ACKNOWLEDGEMENTS

My thanks to all those that have provided permission to reproduce images and for help with research – Cornish Studies Library, Cornwall Council, Oxford Brookes University, the Oxford Centre for Methodism and Church History, Bude-Stratton Town Council, Royal Institution of Cornwall and the Royal Cornwall Museum.

1

ANCIENT CORNWALL

BC TO THE ROMANS

ONCE UPON A TIME

Cornwall has existed – if not by name – for a long time, but there is little evidence available to be able to state exactly when the first people started to reside in the county, let alone reveal what they got up to.

It is thanks to the finds of archaeologists that we can even begin to try to give a date as to when people started to make their home in Cornwall. Certainly, historians have concluded that folk were slow in discovering the delights of the county. Land east of the River Tamar – the natural border between Cornwall and Devon – was settled much earlier, and it is thought that the first to tread on Cornish soil were visitors who did not choose to stay.

At some point during the New Stone Age, people at last started to make Cornwall their place of residence. Over time, more and more seemingly came in search of the tin that was to become so important to future generations, and more and more decided to stay.

There is certainly plenty of evidence of habitation during the New Stone Age, also known as the Neolithic Period. Many megalithic monuments from this era still stand. Burial chambers, known as quoits or dolmens, are examples of the earliest architecture in Cornwall known to us. Formed by a number of upright megaliths supporting a horizontal capstone, it is believed they date to about 3000 BC. The majority can be found in the west of the county, Lanyon Quoit, north of Penzance, being the most famous. Carn Brea, the hilltop site in Redruth, is one of many other places providing further evidence of Neolithic activity.

The Bronze Age saw the move from stone to metal. Bronze is, of course, the alloy of tin and copper; two natural resources that Cornwall is blessed with. It meant that the Cornish tin trade started to flourish, with merchants arriving from all over Europe, most notably the Mediterranean.

Standing stones (menhirs) and stone circles seemingly satisfied the religious needs of the people, and might also have been erected to track the movement of the sun and the

Lanyon Quoit.

moon. Their appearance perhaps highlights the fact that it was not all about survival at this point, an indication that farming was flourishing, or that the people were at least getting enough food to be able to devote time and energy to satisfying more than their basic survival needs.

It is believed stone circles started to appear in Cornwall during the Neolithic Period, but construction of these sites peaked during the early Bronze Age. There are many Bronze Age sites still in evidence in Cornwall, including the Merry Maidens near St Buryan in the far west of the county.

The Iron Age proved to be another boost to agriculture, the new metal being used to make tougher tools that helped increase productivity. Cornwall is home to one of the best examples of an Iron Age village in the whole of the country: Chysauster, near Newmill, Penzance. Castle-an-Dinas, near St Columb Major, is also one of the most impressive hillforts of the era still in evidence. However, it was the dwellers themselves – not their buildings – that really shaped the future of Cornwall. These Iron Age people are, of course, more commonly known as the Celts.

MAKE YOUR PRESENCE 'CELT'
Of all the various settlers in Cornwall, it was the Celts who left the biggest mark on the county. Their greatest legacy was the Cornish language itself.

Historians have long debated the origin of the Celts and are unable to pinpoint an exact time when they first came to Britain. It is suggested that they emerged from Eastern Europe, spreading west from about 1200 BC, at a time when tribal clashes had resulted in much unrest on the Continent. However, some suggest they came earlier and some say later.

It is just as difficult to conclude when the Celts arrived in Cornwall. It is believed a small number first started to filter into the native population during the Bronze Age, though it was probably not until the Iron Age that the Celts reached the peak of their colonisation of the county.

As the Celts mingled with the natives, a number of different dialects gradually fused into one from which the Cornish language was ultimately descended.

It appears people of the Iron Age – or Celts if you prefer – lived well and were generally a civil bunch. Greek geographer Pytheas spoke well of them at any rate.

THOSE NICE CORNISH PEOPLE
The first person to write about Cornwall had good things to say about its people.

Explorer Pytheas, a member of the Greek colony of what is now Marseille in France, is accredited with the first ever written account of Britain, which just happened to be on Cornwall to be precise, ensuring it became the first county to be recorded in writing.

Pytheas came to British shores to trade in about 325 BC. His own account of the voyage has been lost, and we only learn of his observations on the people of Cornwall through later writers quoting extracts from his work. These include historian Diodorus Siculus, who lived more than 200 years after Pytheas.

Through the work of Pytheas – presumed to be quoted or paraphrased by Diodorus – the reader is left in little doubt that tin, with which Cornwall has long been associated, was already a thriving industry.

Pytheas observed that the prepared tin was carried to the tidal island of Ictis, which many believe to be St Michael's Mount, where it was sold to merchants and shipped to the Continent. Notably, Pytheas also pointed out that the people were civilised in manner and hospitable to strangers.

The Cornish will say that nothing has changed in more than 2,000 years.

WHAT'S IN A NAME?
Cornwall has been known by many names. It was Pytheas or Greek historian Diodorus Siculus who supposedly gave it its first one: Belerion.

The name was used by the Greeks, and later by the Romans, to describe the south-western tip of Britain and not necessarily the whole of today's Cornwall.

Belerion is thought to have been the first recorded place name in the United Kingdom. It translates as 'the shining land', which possibly was in reference to the tin found on its shores.

The Celtic kingdom that consisted of what is now Cornwall, Devon and some parts of Somerset and Dorset was named Dumnonia by the Romans.

The name Cornwall (or Kernow in Cornish) is thought to have its origins in a tribe known as the Cornovii that occupied the far west of Dumnonia. The prefix 'corn' or 'kern' means a horn and is most likely in reference to the people being situated at the 'horn' of Britain – the Cornish peninsula. Over time, that area became known as Cornubia, before the Anglo-Saxons added the suffix 'wealas', meaning foreigner, the Cornish people once being known as the 'West Welsh' and effectively occupying the far end of Wales or 'Corn-wealas'.

Cornish antiquarian Richard Carew, famous for *The Survey of Cornwall*, published in 1602, was among those who tried to sum it all up. He put forward this theory:

> Cornwall being cast out into the sea, with the shape of a horn, borrowed the one part of her name from her fashion ... and the other from her inhabitants, both which conjoined make Cornuwalliae, and contrived, Cornwall: in which sense the Cornish people call it Kernow, derived likewise from Kerne, a horn.

Of course, it has to be said that historians have long been trying to find the definitive answer to the question of how Cornwall got its name – and will probably continue to do so for even longer.

CORNWALL WASN'T BUILT IN A DAY

They came, they saw, they conquered.

Well, actually, you could argue that the Romans did not really do that at all in Cornwall.

Yes, they 'came' and yes they 'saw', but, generally, they left the Cornish pretty much to their own devices. Certainly, the influence of Rome, even today, is felt far less in Cornwall than in other counties of England.

Britain was under Roman occupation from AD 43 until the Romans withdrew from the country in AD 410.

However, it appears there was little Roman penetration into Cornwall during these years. The Roman Empire extended westwards, but pretty much stopped in Devon. Exeter, which the Romans called Isca Dumnoniorum, was their most westerly town. It is not really known why the Romans did not, on the whole, venture any further. Some historians have suggested the mass of Dartmoor, still wild country today, put them off.

Tin had put Cornwall on the map, but the tin trade initially declined under Roman rule. The Romans had found an alternative supply in Spain, so had no need to trade with the natives. Had they not gone to Spain for their tin, they might have viewed Cornwall as being of more importance and developed it more than they did. However, when the metal became difficult to obtain in Spain, the Romans of Britain did at last seemingly turn to the rich supply on their own doorstep. Plenty of Roman coins dated between AD 250 and AD 350 have been found in Cornwall, suggesting it was not until then that they really started to tap into its tin industry. However, the Romans had constructed no main roads west of Exeter, meaning that tin had to be shipped out. It is believed the tin trade was pretty much confined to the area west of the Camel and Fowey rivers. And, by the time the tin trade in Cornwall was flourishing again, the best days of the Romans in Britain were coming to an end.

On the whole, it seems that the Cornish did not experience a dramatic change to their way of life under Roman

rule. Throughout the Roman Period, people in Cornwall continued to reside in enclosed settlements, known as rounds, or in courtyard house villages such as Chysauster, just as their Iron Age predecessors had done. A Roman fort existed at Nanstallon, near Bodmin, while traces of two temporary forts near Restormel Castle and Calstock have also recently been unearthed. There is also evidence of a Roman villa at Magor Farm, near Camborne, though it was probably an imitation, built by someone keen to live the Roman way of life.

As well as finds of Roman coins and milestones, that is pretty much it as far as Cornwall is concerned. Some suggest Voliba – as mentioned by famous geographer Ptolemy – may have been a Roman town or settlement somewhere in Cornwall, but the physical evidence of that has yet to come to light. Perhaps more evidence will be found in the future to change the idea that the Romans did not really 'conquer' Cornwall, but until then that is the general view.

The Romans left Britain in AD 410, leaving it open to invasion from other fronts. The Saxons, who had already made inroads into south-east England, were to be next.

Another invasion was also under way. The Romans left us many things, including their religion, and the Christian saints were to come marching in.

2

EARLY
MIDDLE AGES

SAINTS AND SAXONS, KINGS AND VIKINGS

AND DID THOSE FEET IN ANCIENT TIME ...

It took hundreds of years for Christianity to arrive in Cornwall; however, there are some who might argue that Jesus himself came a lot earlier.

There is no historical evidence to prove that Christ came to the county as a teenager under the care of Joseph of Arimathea, but the legend – if that is all that it is – has certainly fired the imagination. William Blake famously posed the question in a poem, which was turned into an even more famous hymn, when he asked: 'And did those feet in ancient time, Walk upon England's mountains green? And was the holy Lamb of God, On England's pleasant pastures seen?'

According to Cornish tradition, Joseph of Arimathea was a wealthy tin merchant who came to Britain to trade. Many places in Cornwall, including St Michael's Mount and St Just in Roseland, claim that he set foot on its soil. Clergyman writer and folklorist Sabine Baring-Gould was among those to spread the idea that Joseph of Arimathea brought the boy Jesus on a trading mission to Cornwall.

WHEN THE SAINTS CAME MARCHING IN

The Cornish have long been making claim to the fact that there are probably more saints in their county than there are in heaven.

In no other county of England have they left such a mark. Many have given their names to towns and villages. You only have to look at a map of Cornwall to be reminded of some of them: St Ives, St Austell, St Agnes ... it goes on.

It is difficult to put a date on when Christianity first arrived in Cornwall. Most historians agree that it was probably not until the late fourth or early fifth century that missionaries, notably from Ireland and Wales, first started coming. However, the conversion of the county was a gradual one and, even during the sixth and seventh centuries – the period that saw the greatest influx of saints – the new faith often existed alongside the old one, rather than replacing it. The earliest Celts were pagans and, for many years to come, superstition sat comfortably alongside Christianity.

Many saints of Cornwall were of royal blood. St Petroc – whose presence at a monastery on the coast for many years played a part in making what is now Padstow the earliest ecclesiastical capital of Cornwall – was the son of a Welsh king. It is said Petroc was responsible for the conversion of Constantine, the sixth-century King of Dumnonia, who was also the successor to King Arthur, according to twelfth-century historian Geoffrey of Monmouth.

Written documentation from the Dark Ages is in short supply. Contemporary accounts of the lives of saints would have been preserved in monasteries that were destroyed by Henry VIII during the Reformation. And those that have survived were written hundreds of years after the arrival of these holy men and women to Cornish shores. It means that their historical accuracy has to be questioned. Often they were also penned to eulogise the founder of a certain religious community and it is probably safe to say that authors such as Geoffrey of Monmouth may have been a bit liberal with the truth. However, few doubt the existence of these missionaries, even if they doubt their miraculous works. In the Celtic Church, people did not need to be canonised to be called a saint and it was usual for all men and women of virtue to be referred to in this way. Many were simply missionaries who did good works, not necessarily miraculous ones. Even so, tales abound of the Cornish saints being a bit special. St Felec (Felix) was able to converse with cats and lions; St Endelienta (Endellion) lived off the milk of a cow, while St Neot was no taller than 4ft and as short as 15in according to some accounts! St Germanus reputedly frightened away invaders by ordering everyone to shout 'Alleluia' in unison, with the result that the confused raiders, believing they were outnumbered and surrounded, dropped their weapons and fled.

Many saints had healing abilities – holy wells often becoming places of pilgrimage. St Keyne gave her name to one of these wells, which was immortalised in a poem by Robert Southey. It is said the well of St Keyne contained water able to grant dominance in a marriage to either husband or wife – depending on which of the newlyweds was first to taste it!

There is, of course, one holy man that is revered above all others in these parts: St Piran, the patron saint of Cornwall.

SAINT AND 'TINNER'

Most visitors to Cornwall arrive via the A30 these days; St Piran came in the fifth century via a quite different route.

It is said that Piran was of Irish origin. He did not, apparently, endear himself to the heathen Irish, for they ended up tying him to a millstone before rolling it off a cliff into the raging sea. It is said that the sea immediately became calm and the millstone, rather than sinking to the depths of the ocean, floated to the surface and carried Piran across the water to the Cornish coastline, landing at what is now Perranporth. Word spread that this newcomer had a gift of performing miracles and soon people from all over were coming to him to be healed.

There are many legends surrounding the lives of the Cornish saints and the true origin of Piran is still unclear. What is certain is that Piran has become the most famous saint in Cornwall. Most accept him to be the patron saint of the county and most accept 5 March as being St Piran's Day, with festivities taking place all over.

St Piran is also the patron saint of tinners and his name has been given to numerous places throughout Cornwall. There is even a mountain in Canada that bears his name, not to mention a small hermit crab found on the Cornish coastline.

However, it is the flag of Cornwall with which St Piran is probably best associated.

FREAK FLAG

Cornwall is not the only county in England to fly a flag, but no other county does so with so much pride and gusto. Indeed, few people outside the duchy would be able to name the colours of their own county flag. And – it is probably safe to say – many outsiders probably know the Cornwall one better. Visitors cannot help but notice that famous image of a white cross on a black background. Flags are flown in gardens, stickers adorn car windows and you can even send one to your friends in the form of a postcard.

The origin of the design for the Cornish flag is unclear. It was adopted as the 'national' flag of Cornwall in the nineteenth century, though there are claims that the design was used many centuries before that. Indeed, its very name – St Piran's flag – suggests a much earlier beginning and puts forward the most romantic theory as to its origin.

St Piran was credited for 'rediscovering' tin in Cornwall – by accident. The Romans had been smelting it for years, but their methods had been lost. It is said that St Piran was using a black hearthstone that – unknown to him – contained tin-bearing ore. In the heat of the hearth, molten tin smelted out of the stone and started to rise to the top, forming a white cross in the process. This remarkable incident supposedly reinvented the tin industry in Cornwall

and earned Piran the accolade of becoming the patron saint of tinners. And, of course, it also gave Cornwall a flag.

Most historians accept that there is, in fact, no evidence to prove that the flag was used any earlier than the first half of the nineteenth century. The earliest known reference to the flag was made by Davies Gilbert in his 1838 work *The Parochial History of Cornwall*. However, despite suggesting the flag was formerly the banner of St Piran and the Standard of Cornwall, it is not clear where he gained his evidence from and he did not leave a record of his research.

There are claims that the design was in use during the Crusades. Others suggest that the Cornish contingent at the Battle of Agincourt displayed it with pride in 1415, though Elizabethan scribe Michael Drayton – in his famous poem *Poly-Olbion* – suggested the Cornish banner at Agincourt depicted two wrestlers in a hitch.

In reality, we are unlikely to ever conclude when the Cornish flag was first flown, but, it is probably safe to say, it is likely to continue flying for many more years to come.

THE MEN WHO WOULD BE KINGS

The history of Cornwall in the Dark Ages is indeed a murky one. It has been clouded by legends and myths.

If the lives of the saints are something of a mystery to us, so too are the lives of the kings of Cornwall, or, to be precise, the kings of Dumnonia – the area consisting of both Cornwall and Devon.

It is also probably not correct to call them kings. In reality, they were probably only chieftains or rulers of small localised areas. There are many names of kings, but little is known about them and it is not known where exactly they ruled. It is impossible to compile a chronological list of these leaders, as many appeared to rule over different people in different areas.

Many suggest that Huwal, or even Cadoc, was the last 'king of Cornwall', the former submitting to the Saxons and the latter to the Normans. Of course, there is one ruler of these lands – if he even existed – that is perhaps shrouded in more mystery than any other.

MUCH SOUGHT 'ARTHUR'

People are often too freely labelled a legend; however, the word was surely conceived for King Arthur. There is no other way to describe him. Everyone knows the name, but no one knows exactly who he was. The legend of King Arthur is, indeed, the ultimate legend.

Cornwall is not the only county to claim Arthur as one of its own. Other places throughout Britain – notably Somerset – also do likewise. But mention King Arthur and most will think of Cornwall.

Of course, some scholars argue Arthur is so much a legend that he does not even deserve a place in any *history* book. Thanks to numerous novels and films, King Arthur appears to be more a work of fiction these days. Indeed, there is no evidence to prove that Arthur ever lived or, if he did, whether he was a king at all.

However, King Arthur cannot be ignored. The popular version of his life – the one that most are familiar with – is the result of the work of Geoffrey of Monmouth, the twelfth-century scribe who penned *The History of the Kings of Britain*. Tourist chiefs in Cornwall certainly have a lot to thank Geoffrey for. He certainly ran with the idea that Cornwall was the home of Arthur and that he met his death in the county. Visitors today are drawn to Slaughterbridge, near Camelford, the spot where Geoffrey of Monmouth claimed Arthur died of his wounds after slaying Mordred.

Cornwall is full of King Arthur associations, some due to Geoffrey of Monmouth and others to those that have taken his story even further. Dozmary Pool on Bodmin Moor is reputed to be the lake into which the sword Excalibur was thrown on the orders of Arthur before he took his last breath. Poet Alfred, Lord Tennyson, in his famous *Idylls of the King*, reputedly chose Loe Pool, near Porthleven, for the sword's resting place.

There is, of course, one place in Cornwall that owes its popularity to the legend of Arthur. Tintagel Castle is named as the place where he was conceived. The castle ruins that attract thousands of visitors these days are Medieval, though the likes of Geoffrey of Monmouth were of the belief that the site was once a seat of royal power.

It is generally accepted that Arthur – if he was real – lived at the end of the fifth or beginning of the sixth century and was at the very least a Celtic leader who led the resistance against the advancing Saxons and other invaders of the time. Geoffrey of Monmouth was not the first to write about Arthur, but his work certainly made him the figure of interest he is today. How much Geoffrey gleaned from earlier sources or made up – his book was imaginative to say the least – is debatable.

According to folklore, Arthur's spirit can be found in the 'national' bird of Cornwall – the chough – its red beak and feet signifying his final bloody battle.

That bird is under threat on Cornish soil. Needless to say, the same cannot be said of King Arthur.

KING DIDN'T HAVE A GOOD 'KNIGHT'

It is perhaps ironic that the most popular Arthurian legend does not actually feature King Arthur.

Another king of Cornwall – Mark – has the honour of playing a part in arguably the world's most famous love triangle.

King Mark, who is said to have lived at the beginning of the sixth century, was not the hero of the tale, however. And it is the names of Tristan and Iseult – the other players in this tragedy – that have gained immortality in Cornwall and beyond.

There are many variations of the legend and no evidence of truth in any of them. The most famous depiction can be found in *Le Morte d'Arthur*, the work of fifteenth-century author Sir Thomas Malory.

Tristan was from Lyonesse, the mythical lost land situated off the tip of Cornwall, or – for the less romantic – possibly an area of Brittany. He was the nephew of King Mark and served the royal court as his knight. It was in Ireland that he met Iseult, the daughter of a king, and it was his intention to bring her back to Cornwall to be the bride of his uncle. However, during the journey, the pair fell in love after ingesting a love potion intended for Mark. They remained lovers even after Mark wed Iseult. However, Mark eventually discovered the truth and set about punishing them. Sentenced to death, Tristan escaped and fled with Iseult. It was not long before they were captured, but Mark agreed to spare the life of Tristan for the return of Iseult. Tristan began a new life back in Lyonesse and married another woman, but was unable to free his mind of Iseult. There are a number of variations on the ultimate fate of Tristan and Iseult, the most romantic being one in which Tristan, wounded during a battle, calls for his true love, the only one he believes can save him. Iseult is summoned and comes to him, but the jealous wife of Tristan deceives him, informing her husband that Iseult is not aboard the incoming mercy ship. Tristan loses the will to live and is dead when Iseult reaches him, and she then herself dying of grief.

Some say that King Mark brought the bodies back to Cornwall and to his chief residence – Castle Dore, near Fowey – the famous Tristan Stone once marking their place of burial.

THE 'SAX' PACK

No one wants to be last, and it can be a nuisance being the 'last' county in England. All through history, the Cornish have often had to wait for things a little longer than the rest of the country. Of course, that is not always a bad thing. Indeed, the Romans took so long to make their mark in Cornwall that they hardly made one in the end. And the same can perhaps be said of the Saxons.

Elsewhere in the country, the Saxons were making noises even before the Romans had withdrawn in AD 410. These new barbarian invaders gradually pushed west, but it was to be a long time before Cornwall submitted to their rule. The Battle of Deorham, near Bristol, in AD 577 had some effect on the West Country, if not specifically Cornwall. The victory for the Saxons resulted in the separation of the Celtic kingdom of Dumnonia (Devon and Cornwall) from Wales, the Dumnonians or Cornish being known as the 'West Welsh' at that time. However, Saxon progress west remained slow. The *Anglo-Saxon Chronicle* states that Centwine, King of Wessex (West Saxons), saw off the Britons as far as the sea in AD 682. But it is not known if those 'Britons' were of Cornish origin or whether that 'sea' was beside what is today the north-east of Cornwall, as some historians have suggested. There is even doubt over where King Geraint of Dumnonia was defeated by Ine, King of Wessex, in AD 710. Some suggest this was the significant moment when Exeter – the most westerly town of significance – fell to the Saxons, while others claim that the invaders had already pushed further west by this time and that the battle was actually fought between the rivers Tamar and Lynher on Cornish soil.

The Dumnonians continued to offer resistance, winning in about AD 722 – with the help of the Welsh – a battle at Hehil, possibly somewhere on the Camel estuary, but more probably in Devon.

Just how far west the Saxons advanced in the eighth century is not clear, but it appears that Cornwall was still allowed to pursue its Celtic way of life, as it had done during the Roman era, and it was not until Egbert, the new leader of the West Saxons, famously invaded Dumnonia again in AD 813 and 'spread devastation in Cornwall from east to west' that even the Cornish rulers had to submit to a new king. Egbert – now with even Cornwall in his control – is often described as the first king of all England.

Even though the heathen Saxons had by now converted to Christianity – following the arrival of St Augustine in Kent – this significant event made little difference to the Cornish. It must not be forgotten that Cornwall's 'Christianity' was still mixed with a huge dose of paganism. The Anglo-Saxons, at the Synod of Whitby in AD 664, had agreed to make the country an ecclesiastical province of Rome, but the Celtic Church of Dumnonia refused to follow suit, ensuring its religious customs and practices were very different from those in the rest of England.

The Cornish continued to fight hard to keep their independence. They had no intention of allowing the barbarians to impose their way of life upon them. They rebelled against the invading Saxons, only to be defeated at possibly Camelford in about AD 825. Some have suggested the battle site at Slaughterbridge, on the outskirts of the town, in fact, commemorates Egbert's victory over the Cornish, rather than King Arthur's triumph over Mordred.

Hope was not lost for the Celtic race and, in AD 838, when a Viking fleet reached the Cornish coast, the opportunist people of Cornwall formed an alliance with these new invaders who had already been making their presence felt elsewhere in the country. Both shared the common goal of trying to rid England of the Saxons. However, Egbert marched west across the River Tamar and, at Hingston Down, near Callington, killed two birds with one stone: the Vikings fled and the Cornish were forced to once again pay homage to their Saxon king.

However, Cornwall was only nominally incorporated into Wessex and still appeared to have its regional rulers. Evidence of that can be found on the remains of a stone cross at St Cleer, near Liskeard, which honours a Cornish 'king' named Doniert, who did not die until as late as AD 875, when he drowned in the River Fowey.

There is much evidence of Saxon colonisation in the east of the county through a large number of places, such as Stratton, Poundstock and Crackington Haven, whose names are Saxon in origin, though it was not until the late ninth century that Saxon influence was felt in mid Cornwall. As for the far west, it remained almost untouched. The many Viking raids kept the Saxons occupied and, for those in the far west of Cornwall, the Saxon conquest probably meant very little.

It was not until the reign of Athelstan that all of Cornwall was absorbed into a new united kingdom of England. However, in famously fixing the River Tamar to be the border between Cornwall and the rest of the country, some claim that Athelstan merely succeeded in further *disuniting* the Cornish.

THEM AND US

It appears that King Athelstan did not like the people of Cornwall. He made it illegal for a Cornishman to own land in England and legal for Englishmen to kill the Cornish, including women and children.

According to William of Malmesbury, writing in the twelfth century, Athelstan attacked the Cornish, or Dumnonians as they were then still known, 'with great energy, compelling them to withdraw from Exeter, which until that time they had inhabited on a footing of legal equality with the English'.

The Cornish were driven further west, Athelstan making it clear to them that the River Tamar was the border, and that it would not be to their advantage should they cross it. And so, as William of Malmesbury rather bluntly put it, Athelstan 'cleansed the city [Exeter] of its defilement by wiping out that filthy race'.

Of course, that was not strictly true. The Cornish were merely shifted further west. The new border created the Cornwall, in territorial and political terms, that still exists today.

Athelstan is often described as the first true king of all England, though others, including Egbert and even Alfred the Great, the grandfather of Athelstan, are sometimes given this title. However, Athelstan made it clear that he was now in charge of *all* the country. According to the *Anglo-Saxon Chronicle*, Huwal – the ruler of Cornwall – was allowed to continue to go about his business, so long as he recognised that Athelstan was really the one in charge. With Athelstan as overlord of his Celtic neighbours, it effectively made Huwal the last true 'king of Cornwall'. There is no evidence to suggest that Athelstan broke his side of the bargain and the Cornish did not come under further attack, the English seemingly content to leave them to their own devices.

Subsequent kings of England seemed happy to continue with this arrangement. It meant Cornwall, despite being under the influence of England, pretty much retained its independence. King Edgar, for example, called himself king of the English and ruler of the adjacent nations, while Aethelred described Cornwall not as a shire of England, but a province. It is quite clear that Cornwall was still not part of the rest of the country.

VIKINGS 'HORN' IN ON THE PARTY

It appears Cornwall got off lightly under the Vikings as well. Repeated Viking raids caused mayhem throughout England, but the Cornish were again largely left alone.

The most famous Viking attack in Cornwall took place in AD 981, according to the *Anglo-Saxon Chronicle*, when what is now Padstow was pretty much laid to waste.

For a spell in the first half of the eleventh century, England came under Danish rule, but it had little effect on Cornwall. Sweyn Forkbeard added the region of Wessex to his growing empire after crushing the Saxons in about

1013, but he allowed Cornwall self-rule in return for an annual payment. King Canute, who ruled England from 1016 to 1035, also appeared to leave the Cornish to get on with their own business, Cornwall not being included in the list of his territories.

Incredibly, for the first thousand years or so following the birth of Christ, Cornwall had somehow largely escaped from the influence of all the major invaders of Britain: the Romans, Saxons and Vikings. However, there was no escape from the next and last successful military invaders of England – the Normans.

3

HIGH AND LATE MIDDLE AGES

EARLS AND DUKES

THE NEW 'NORM'

It is perhaps no surprise to learn that the Cornish were among the last in England to submit to the Normans. Indeed, it took William the Conqueror longer than he probably would have liked to 'conquer' Cornwall.

It was almost two years before the new king – following his victory at the Battle of Hastings in 1066 – marched into the county. There remained much resistance to the invaders and William had come fresh from dealing with a revolt at Exeter.

However, once the Normans had set foot in this remote part of their new kingdom, they wasted no time in completing the subjugation of south-west England.

To say that the Normans left their mark in Cornwall would be an understatement. It was during the Norman era that Cornwall started to become integrated into Britain. Under the Saxons, Cornwall was still almost a foreign country, pretty much left to its own devices. The Normans had no intention of letting it remain so. William knew that

Launceston Castle.

he would be more powerful – and richer – if all the land was under his control.

Indeed, Cornwall must have been an important part of his plans, as he gave most of it to his trusted half-brother, Robert, Count of Mortain. The count, as he was known, is described by many as the first Earl of Cornwall, though it is thought he never actually assumed that title. He became the greatest landowner in all England after the king. He held hundreds of English manors, many in the south-west, particularly Cornwall. Robert of Mortain certainly left his mark. He and his successors were responsible for the building of some of Cornwall's most famous castles: Launceston, Restormel, Tintagel and Trematon. They all differ from the later forts of Henry VIII, such as Pendennis and St Mawes, in that they were not constructed solely for the purpose of defence. They served as administrative centres, places where the Normans could manage and control their newly acquired territory.

The first Norman castle was built at Launceston. Robert of Mortain decided to make it his headquarters and the town became the first 'capital' of Cornwall.

OUR SURVEY SAID ...

It was the Normans who carried out the Great Survey of 1086. *The Domesday Book*, the result of that survey, offers a glimpse of what Cornwall was like during the eleventh century, but it does not provide a complete picture of life in the county. From it, one can conclude that many inhabitants of Cornwall lived in great poverty, though that is perhaps no surprise. It does also remind us of how sparse the population was. Bodmin, the biggest town at the time of the survey, had fewer than 100 houses. The major landowner of the time was, unsurprisingly, Robert of Mortain. It reveals that he was in possession of more than three-quarters of the 300-plus Cornish manors.

The Domesday Book names Turstin as High Sheriff of Cornwall, the earliest known incumbent of this important role.

GIVE THEM 'EARL'

There has been much debate as to who had the honour of being the first Earl of Cornwall, a role created by the Normans.

Some scholars have given the title to Cadoc, who, if he was not the last 'king' of Cornwall, as some suppose, was at least in some position of power at the time of the Norman Conquest. It would therefore perhaps make sense for King William to make him his first Earl of Cornwall, as fifteenth-century chronicler William of Worcester believed to be the case. Other historians claim Brian of Brittany was handed the role in preference to Cadoc.

By the mid-twelfth century the office was generally bestowed upon a member of the royal family. The earldom had to be recreated several times over the years before the position was reinvented as the Duchy of Cornwall.

The last Earl of Cornwall to reside in the county was Edmund. He built the Duchy Palace at Lostwithiel at the end of the thirteenth century. It became the administrative centre of first the earldom and then the reinvented Duchy of Cornwall. It effectively made Lostwithiel the capital of the county.

ONE AND ALL
A story in the life of one former Earl of Cornwall is supposedly reflected on the current duchy coat of arms.

The black shield contains fifteen gold discs forming the shape of a triangle. It is said that they represent the coins that were needed to pay a ransom for the safe return of Richard, 1st Earl of Cornwall, who was reputedly captured by the Saracens during the Crusades in the thirteenth century. The Cornish motto 'one and all' signifies the joint effort made by the people of Cornwall in raising the cash to save their earl. It is a fanciful story and, it has to be said, there are other versions as to how the county got the design for its arms, but the motto, in particular, is still much quoted today to emphasise community spirit in Cornwall.

Richard – whose dream was to become emperor of the Holy Roman Empire – was given Cornwall as a birthday present from elder brother Henry III. The earl built the present castle at Tintagel and granted Launceston free borough status, allowing the people to build a guildhall … in return for an annual fee of a pound of pepper!

CROWN 'DUELS'

One man of royal blood who held the position of Earl of Cornwall in its early days was to become engulfed in one of the most troubled times in British history.

Reginald de Dunstanville was the illegitimate son of Henry I. The death of his father in 1135 brought an end to the relative order and stability enjoyed during the first half of Norman rule. Two contenders for the throne emerged. Matilda was the daughter of Henry and his choice to succeed him. However, the barons crowned Stephen, the nephew of Henry and grandson of William the Conqueror.

For a decade or so, the nation was divided. The civil war was felt in Cornwall and Reginald de Dunstanville was at the heart of it. It is said that he switched his allegiance from Stephen to Matilda. Some historians suggest that it was not Stephen who appointed Reginald in the role of Earl of Cornwall. Instead, they claim that it was Reginald's father-in-law, William Fitz Richard of Cardinham – a Cornish nobleman and another defector – who persuaded him to *unofficially* take up the position, only for Reginald to be kicked out of Launceston Castle when an angry Stephen sent an army to sort out the rebels. It is said that Reginald did return to secure Cornwall and, of course, the supporters of Matilda eventually had the last laugh, her son – Henry II – finally becoming king following the death of Stephen.

'TIN' MONEY

You could say that Cornwall officially took the law into its own hands at the beginning of the thirteenth century.

In the eyes of many, it was still a foreign country – despite continued Norman attempts to integrate it into the rest of England – and its uniqueness was only emphasised further by the introduction of stannary charters.

In Latin 'stannum' is the word for tin. Stannaries were simply districts where tin was mined. The tin industry was big business and had been thriving for a long time. As a result, it had its own laws and customs that had been handed

down the generations. King John, in 1201, effectively confirmed that Cornwall was a law unto itself when he issued
the first stannary charter, setting out the ancient rights
and privileges of tinners in a legal document. It exempted
tinners from the normal laws and taxes of the country.
Notably, it allowed the people of Cornwall to search for
tin on common ground, without hindrance from any man.
Effectively, anyone was able to mine on unenclosed land.
This practice of 'bounding' dated back to pre-Christian
times. A miner could claim a piece of ground for his own
to mine and then mark it to keep others away. It meant the
poorest miner could search for tin, provided he registered
his 'bounds' (boundaries) with the stannary court.

Further charters followed the first one issued by King
John. Henry III confirmed the charter of his father and
Edward I strengthened the rights of Cornish tinners with
another at the beginning of the fourteenth century.

Of course, the tinners had duties to perform in return for
the legalisation of their rights and privileges. For administrative purposes, Cornwall was divided into four stannaries.
Each had its own court. The Stannary Palace at Lostwithiel,
later known as the Duchy Palace, became home to the
Stannary Parliament, which served Cornwall just like the
one at Westminster served the rest of the country. There
was even a prison for those who broke stannary laws. The
stannaries ultimately came under the control of the residing
Earl of Cornwall and then the Duke of Cornwall after the
earldom became a duchy.

The tinners in Cornwall continued to live and work
subject to the laws of the stannaries. Only when orders of
the king were issued through the stannary warden did the
miners have to obey their monarch.

The stannaries played a part in preserving the independence of Cornwall, but, in a way, their creation also brought
the county closer to the rest of the country. In bowing to the
desires of the Cornish, the king was really also satisfying his
own. He may have been prepared to let the Cornish tinners

do as they had done for centuries, but it would come at a price.

THE FIRST SMUGGLERS

Cornwall is smuggling country. All kinds of goods have been smuggled into the county over the years; however, some items were smuggled *out*.

Tin smuggling was rife. Just as there is often a tax to be paid on goods arriving into the county, the tinners had to pay a tax before their tin was able to leave it. And, of course, few like paying taxes. It is said the Cornish paid a higher tax than neighbours in Devon because the Cornish were 'foreigners'.

The stannary charters made it easier for the monarch to control and regulate the tin industry. In other words, he made sure that he got his share of the profits. It became more difficult for tinners to get their tin out of the county before being 'coined'.

Each stannary had a coinage town. These were the administrative centres where the tin was taken before being sold. The term 'coinage' has nothing to do with money, but originates from the French word *coin* – meaning corner. Before being given the mark of approval, a corner of the tin was cut off and tested to ensure it was of good quality. All tin had to pass through the coinage process and, crucially, it could only be sold after the tax had been collected on it.

ABLE TO TAKE A 'DUKE'

Many regard 1337 as being the most significant year in Cornish history. The independence of the county was effectively confirmed in that year – in the creation of the Duchy of Cornwall.

Edward III, in regenerating the earldom of Cornwall into a duchy, was making it clear that even he recognised that the county was like no other.

Cornwall has always been largely independent from the rest of the country. It has always had its own rulers – from the early kings to its earls – while the stannary charters had also confirmed its right to have its own government and laws. The stannary courts formed what was effectively the first independent legal system in England. However, in proclaiming his son as the first Duke of Cornwall, Edward III was *constitutionally* confirming the semi-independence of the county.

The title has been passed on to the eldest son of every subsequent monarch. The Duchy of Cornwall became – and still is – a chief source of income for the heir to the throne. The son of Edward III – Edward, the Black Prince – was just seven when he was appointed first Duke of Cornwall. There were many financial benefits, including his right to collect a duty of £2 on every 1,000lb of tin. And that would have bought a lot of toys!

GAME OF THRONES

Edward III had his sights on a bigger crown than the Cornish one. He was happy for his son and the heirs of subsequent monarchs to 'rule' Cornwall, but he would not give up his claim to the throne of France so easily. In the same year that he created the Duchy of Cornwall, Edward III officially commenced his campaign to become king across the Channel, following the outbreak of the Hundred Years' War.

In fact, Cornwall contributed much during the hostilities. Cornish tin helped fund the Battle of Crécy, while its ports supplied both men and ships. Sir John Treffry of Fowey was among those who fought alongside the first Duke of Cornwall – the Black Prince. During the Battle of Poitiers, Treffry famously captured the French flag. For his reward, he was knighted on the battlefield and permitted to use the French royal emblem on his own coat of arms.

Fowey, being the principal Cornish port in the fourteenth century, provided more ships than any other town in England for the Siege of Calais. As a reward, the port was given permission to freely raid and seize French ships in the

Channel, an undertaking the Fowey Gallants – a group of privateers – took on with relish, earning quite a reputation in the process. Even when the war with France was over, the attacks did not cease.

However, the French got their revenge on Fowey in 1457, when they ransacked the port, taking advantage of the fact that most of the men were away at sea. However, they still met a formidable opponent in Elizabeth Treffry, who reputedly sent them packing by pouring molten lead over the marauders when they reached her manor house.

BLACK DAYS

It is a wonder that there was anyone left to fight the French during the second half of the fourteenth century. The Black Death, which arrived in 1348, is said to have wiped out almost half the population of England.

It reached Cornwall in the spring of 1349. Compared to other parts of the country, it is believed Cornwall got off lightly, with just a mere third of its population wiped out.

NOT PLEASANT TO THE PEASANT

The famous Peasants' Revolt of 1381 took place chiefly in the south-east of England, and it was to be another 100-plus years before the people of Cornwall took up arms against the government, An Gof's Cornish rebellion taking place in 1497.

However, Cornwall – or at least a Cornishman – had a big role to play in the Peasants' Revolt, the most famous uprising in British history. It was not a role many would have enjoyed to play and Sir Robert Tresilian – the man who did so – became one of the most unpopular figures in England.

Tresilian had risen to Lord Chief Justice and one of his jobs following the failed Peasants' Revolt was punishing the rebels. It was definitely the 'baddie' role – at least in the eyes of the ordinary man on the street. Most believed the revolt, which had its roots primarily in Essex and Kent, was justified. The Hundred Years' War with France was proving costly to the country and the king needed to boost the coffers. Unfortunately, the long-suffering people did not have the means to pay the higher taxes and marched to London to make it clear that they had had enough.

After the dust had settled, the rebels were rounded up. Tresilian showed little mercy towards the culprits. There are many claims that he went outside the law to ensure 'justice' was done. It is said that he trumped up charges and pressured jurors.

Tresilian remained loyal to Richard II, but his opponents were to have the last laugh. A group of nobles known as the Lords Appellant had him executed for treason.

4

EARLY TUDOR

ROSES, REBELLION AND REFORMATION

RED OR WHITE?

Cornwall did not play a major role in the Wars of the Roses. The Cornish peasant could have got on with life pretty much as normal. It was the gentry who had more to win or lose, and most of the leading Cornish families became caught up in the ultimate battle for the throne of England.

The mid-fifteenth century was a time of anarchy. Noble families up and down the country became involved in local struggles for power with their neighbours, having little regard for royal authority and the law. Cornwall had a small part to play in one of these private wars – the most famous one in the south-west – which was between two feuding families from Devon. The powerful Courtenays and Bonvilles had been at loggerheads for years. Their feud blew up after Henry VI agreed to appoint William Bonville to the lucrative position of stewardship of the Duchy of Cornwall. However, Thomas Courtenay later insisted that he was the man for the job and Henry, ignoring his earlier appointment of a Bonville, seemingly agreed. With the Bonvilles and Courtenays already not seeing eye to eye, a job share was not an option, with the result that the two

families went to war in
a bid to sort out their
differences.

Similar strug-
gles for local
dominance took
place throughout the
country, playing alongside
the biggest struggle of
all – for the throne
of England itself.
Henry VI, of the
House of Lancaster,
was a weak king, and those
of the House of York saw it
as their chance to revive their
claim to the throne. Local battles
between families became intertwined
with the national conflict, their fortunes very much dependent on which
colour rose they wore: the red of the Lancastrians or the
white of the Yorkists.

Most Cornish families supported the Lancastrians.
However, following the Battle of Barnet and death of
Henry VI, the game looked up for them. Edward IV was
on the throne and the Yorkists were to hold on to it until
Richard III was defeated at Bosworth. The last forlorn
Lancastrian revolt against Edward IV (until Bosworth) had
taken place on the coast of Cornwall.

I *DON'T* LIKE TO BE BESIDE THE SEASIDE
Many people love Cornwall for the fact that you are never
far from a beach. However, that became a problem for
Yorkist Sir John Arundell. It is said that a curse was placed
on him: 'When upon the yellow sand, thou shall die by
human hand.'

And so when his Yorkist king – Edward IV – ordered him to the vast beach at Marazion to recapture St Michael's Mount from the Lancastrians, you could have forgiven Arundell for being a little concerned. Indeed, it is said he was so fearful of the curse that he avoided beaches and even moved to a house far from the sea.

It was the arrival of the Earl of Oxford in Cornwall in the early 1470s that made a trip to the seaside necessary for Arundell. Oxford, a loyal supporter of Henry Tudor – the Lancastrian claimant to the throne – had sailed into Mount's Bay and, disguised as pilgrims, he and his men had taken over the monastery on the island. Edward was not impressed and ordered the Sheriff of Cornwall – none other than Arundell – to see off Oxford. Arundell had no choice but to obey the king and went into battle. And, you will not be surprised to learn, the poor knight was killed – on the 'yellow sand' of Marazion Beach. It is a fanciful story and many believe it to be more a work of fiction than fact.

Fortunately, the successor of Arundell – John Fortescue – did not share a mistrust of beaches, but, at any rate, came up with a plan that would not involve him having to do battle anywhere. Indeed, the new Sheriff of Cornwall came up with a better idea to rid St Michael's Mount of

St Michael's Mount.

the unwanted guests. He besieged the island and cut off all escape routes. He then attempted to get the Lancastrians to surrender. Rather than goading them into battle, the shrewd Fortescue tried to win over the Lancastrian soldiers. He kept in contact with those on the island, promising them a full pardon and land if they gave up their arms. Gradually, over the next six months or so, more and more Lancastrians took up his offer. With only a handful of men left, Oxford had no choice but to surrender.

Oxford was imprisoned in France, but later escaped and joined Henry Tudor. And it was not until 1485 that they returned to England to triumph at Bosworth and thereby restore the House of Lancaster to the English throne.

RUN FOR THE ROSES
The greatest rivals in Cornwall during the Wars of the Roses had to be quick on their feet. Both had to flee for their lives at the hand of the other on separate occasions – with the result that both got away in dramatic circumstances.

Sir Henry Bodrugan was the leading Yorkist in the county, while Sir Richard Edgcumbe could claim the same title among the Lancastrians. Needless to say, they did not get on.

Bodrugan was the first to give his foe some exercise. Despite having a reputation for being a pirate and a man of violence, he was one of the most powerful and influential men in Cornwall. As a supporter of Richard III – who was crowned in 1483 – Bodrugan took on the job of rounding up his leading Lancastrian opponents, including Edgcumbe. It is said that Edgcumbe was chased through the woods of his own home at Cotehele, near Calstock. When he reached the River Tamar, Edgcumbe threw his hat into the water. Bodrugan is said to have seen the hat floating by and wrongly presumed his arch-enemy had drowned. Richard rewarded Bodrugan and other Cornish supporters of the House of York with land once belonging to the defeated Lancastrians. However, the 'reds' were to fight back. Edgcumbe eventually escaped to join Henry Tudor – the Lancastrian claimant to the throne – in exile in Brittany and, in 1485, they returned to defeat Richard at Bosworth, their leader crowned Henry VII.

With the House of Lancaster restored to the throne, it was time for the Yorkists to flee for their lives. No doubt Edgcumbe would have relished the opportunity to see his rival out of Cornwall and take his lands. It is said that Bodrugan was chased to Turbot Point above Colona Beach, near Gorran Haven, and there, still on his horse, leapt off the cliff into the sea. A waiting boat picked him up and he went on to begin a new life abroad. That cliff is still known today as Bodrugan's Leap.

However, now that he was on the throne, Henry VII did not exactly endear himself to the Cornish. In fact, it was not long before they were up in arms against him.

HE MADE A NAME FOR HIMSELF

Michael Joseph – shortly before his death – declared that his name would be remembered forever.

Most outside Cornwall probably shake their heads in bemusement when it is put to them. And even in the county, that name may not provoke much of a response. However, refer to the man by his nickname and almost every Cornishman or woman will know who you are talking about. In fact, the name 'An Gof' is one that most Cornish residents will say with pride – the humble blacksmith who took upon the establishment, becoming, to many, a true hero of Cornwall.

Michael An Gof – his nickname translates as 'the black-smith' – was the leader of the Cornish rebellion of 1497, the most famous uprising in Cornish history.

Henry VII – who took to the throne following the end of the Wars of the Roses – was short of cash. And, needing more of it to finance his army preparing to fight the Scots, he introduced a tax that caused much anger and contro-versy. The tax was a national one, but the Cornish found the idea harder to swallow than the rest of England. In fact, An Gof was not prepared to swallow it, and set about getting the king to change his mind. It is incredible to think that tiny St Keverne on the Lizard peninsula – where An Gof plied his trade – should become the starting point of an incredible journey.

An Gof – along with fellow leader Thomas Flamank who joined the rebellion at Bodmin – led some 15,000 rebels on a march to London. More insurgents joined in Devon and Somerset, but it was chiefly Cornishmen who set out to put pressure on the king to change his mind. Many have come up with suggestions as to why Cornwall, in particular, was so riled by the tax. Of course, most Cornishmen were already poor and no one likes paying taxes, especially to fund a war a very long way from the duchy. However, the very poorest were excused from the new tax and some suggest that the real reason why An Gof and others were so full of fury was because of their hatred of the local tax collector – the merciless Sir John Oby, provost of Glasney College in Penryn. Some historians say that it was pride that sparked the flame.

The rebels had little chance of success. On arrival in London, they found themselves up against the army that had been set up to defeat the Scots, it having not yet started its journey north. An Gof and Flamank hoped to gain extra support from the people of Kent, who had rallied during the more famous Peasants' Revolt of 1381, but to no joy.

The rebellion was eventually quashed at Blackheath. An Gof and Flamank were two of those who died for the cause. Both were convicted of treason and executed.

The courageous An Gof, before his execution, insisted his name would live on and added that he would gain 'a fame permanent and immortal'.

Certainly, in Cornwall at least, An Gof appears to have achieved that.

HERE WE GO AGAIN!

You would have thought that the Cornish would have learned their lesson after witnessing the fate of rebels An Gof and Thomas Flamank.

However, only a few months had passed since those two agitators were put to death for their part in the Cornish rebellion of 1497 when more disgruntled Cornishmen were preparing to take up arms. This time their leader was an outsider – Perkin Warbeck, a pretender to the throne, who claimed that he was one of the two young princes supposedly murdered in the Tower of London. He came to Cornwall to rally support, reputedly landing at Whitesand Bay, near Land's End. Still disillusioned with their lot in life, some 6,000 Cornish rebels set off with Warbeck.

However, they did not get as far as An Gof and Flamank, reaching only Somerset. Warbeck, it appears, lost his nerve and did a runner, abandoning his bemused and angry followers.

You could not blame Henry VII for being less than impressed with the Cornish. However, fearing further uprisings, he made the county pay for the rebellion only in monetary terms, issuing fines – rather than death sentences – to the perpetrators.

KING OF THE CASTLE

You would expect the most famous King of England to leave his mark on Cornwall, and no part of Britain – or indeed Europe – could fail to be affected by the reign of Henry VIII.

The Reformation did not only bring political and religious changes, but physical ones. The very landscape of Cornwall was transformed because of the consequences of England breaking from the Church of Rome.

Henry set about pulling down buildings and putting up others. Down went the religious houses during the Dissolution of the Monasteries from 1536, the king making

Henry VIII.

it clear that the Catholic Church no longer had any power in England.

However, in breaking all ties with Rome, Henry made more enemies. And that meant the threat of war. Henry set to work on building a series of forts along the south coast of England, including Cornwall, to protect the country from the real threat of invasion from Catholic Europe.

Two of the most famous castles in Cornwall are the legacy of this troubled period in our history. Pendennis Castle – the largest in the county – and St Mawes Castle sit opposite each other, guarding Carrick Roads, the estuary of the River Fal. Both have been modified over the years. Pendennis, in particular, is very different from the one built by Henry, though St Mawes saw little development after its original construction.

OVER HIS DEAD 'BODY'!

There must have been something in the air at St Keverne. Some fifty years after An Gof had famously inspired the Cornish rebellion of 1497, another resident of that village on the Lizard peninsula was at the centre of yet another uprising.

Martin Geoffrey was the priest at St Keverne, one of many residents of Cornwall who did not approve of the Protestant Reformation. Indeed, most of the county was not in favour of it. Catholicism was an important part of Cornish culture. Many traditions and customs in Cornwall were associated with the Catholic religion: the celebration of saints' days and feasts, as well as the care of holy wells and shrines. Many felt that the very culture of Cornwall would be destroyed under the new Church of England. The Catholic Church had also accommodated the Cornish language, but, with the removal of monastic education, many were of the belief that the very independence of Cornwall was now under threat. The famous Glasney College at Penryn was among the religious centres that fell during and after the Dissolution of the Monasteries. It is believed that fourteenth-century Cornish translator John Trevisa was a former pupil. Trevisa would have spoken the Cornish tongue at Glasney, so it is perhaps ironic that his translations from Latin into Middle English helped develop the English language we have now, and at the same time played a part in the demise of the Cornish tongue.

The fall of Glasney and other similar Catholic institutions would certainly have riled traditional Catholics. The last straw for Martin Geoffrey, however, was the arrival from London of a man named William Body. He came to further promote the new Protestant religion. His task was to remove the many Catholic symbols from Cornwall: religious statues, images and monuments.

When Body arrived in Helston in 1548, he set about desecrating the parish church. News of what he was doing reached residents in the surrounding villages. Some 1,000 people, led by Geoffrey, marched to Helston to put a stop to Body. Knowing that an angry mob was on its way, Body took shelter in a nearby house, but his hiding place was discovered and he was dragged outside. The crowd showed no mercy and Body was stabbed to death.

Still defiant, the mob increased in numbers and it is said about 3,000 people in Helston took up arms, determined not to let the government investigate the death of Body. The ministers of Edward VI – he was too young to make any decisions himself – feared the army would grow even larger and lead to rebellion. They paid Cornishmen from the east of the county to try to persuade their neighbours to put down their arms.

In the end, a number of rebels were arrested for the murder of Body. Some of them were pardoned, but others – including Martin Geoffrey – were not so lucky, the priest of St Keverne being taken to London to be executed.

One of the rebels was purposely executed at Plymouth in Devon. The idea was to warn Devonians of the consequences should they also try to oppose the Protestant Reformation. It did not work. In the following year, Devon had joined Cornwall in rising up against the new Church of England.

SORRY SEEMS TO BE THE HARDEST WORD

It took a long time for the Church of England to apologise for its role in the Prayer Book Rebellion – more than 450 years, in fact.

In 2007, the Bishop of Truro publicly denounced the actions of the government that resulted in the deaths of many unarmed Cornishmen.

The Prayer Book Rebellion of 1549 was evidence that the people of Devon and Cornwall still remained loyal to the Catholic Church. The executions of key rebels involved in the murder of William Body at Helston in the previous year were not enough to keep the people quiet.

It is wrong to say that the introduction of the *Book of Common Prayer* was the only reason for the latest uprising, but for many it was certainly the last straw.

All churches throughout the country were ordered to use the new English prayer book. However, many in Cornwall could only speak Cornish and this was another threat to their language, as well as another significant change to the way they had worshiped God.

Humphrey Arundell and John Winslade were the leaders of the Cornish rebels. Angry over the intention to rid the country of all Catholic practices, they planned to march all the way to London to make their point.

A number of manor houses and castles in Cornwall were captured as the rebels – whose ranks included Cornish clergymen – made sport of their gentry opponents as they headed east. The influential Sir Richard Grenville, the former Sheriff of Cornwall, was among those apprehended and then imprisoned at Launceston. Supporters from Devon swelled the rebel numbers.

A number of bloody battles took place around the Exeter area. It was at Clyst Heath that hundreds of unarmed Cornish prisoners were brutally killed. It did not stop there. Many of the rebel leaders were executed and, even when the rebellion had been quashed, the government, led by the cruel Sir Anthony Kingston, took pains to seek out others it believed were still a threat. At least one Cornish vicar was hanged from his church tower. It was a bloody and shameful episode in British history.

The fact that the Right Reverend Bill Ind – fondly viewed as a bishop of the people – felt the need to issue an apology on behalf of the government and Church of England in 2007, so long after the event, is evidence that the Cornish have never forgotten it and maybe never will.

KEEP THE FAITH

The hopes of Catholics in Cornwall rose when Mary I took to the throne in 1553. 'Bloody Mary' – the nickname she earned for her relentless persecution of Protestants – made it her mission to undo the new Church of England and restore Catholicism.

However, her reign lasted only five years. And, when her half-sister, Elizabeth, took to the throne in 1558, the new monarch restored Protestantism as the religion of England.

Elizabeth I was not as intolerant towards Catholics as Mary had been towards Protestants, but there was still blood on her hands. And Cornwall has the unenviable distinction of being the location of the first execution of a Catholic seminary priest during her reign.

Devon-born Cuthbert Mayne was executed at Launceston in 1577. He was arrested at the home of Catholic sympathiser Francis Tregian, a relation of the Arundells. The Sheriff of Cornwall, another Sir Richard Grenville, conducted a raid on Tregian's house at Probus. Mayne, who had lived in the Tregian household under the guise of a steward, was held in Launceston Castle for three months following his arrest. Various charges were brought before him, including celebrating mass in the papal manner. He was informed that his life would be spared if he renounced his Catholicism and acknowledged Elizabeth as the head of the Church, but Mayne refused to do so. He was dragged through the streets of Launceston and executed.

It was not just Catholics who suffered for their faith. Almost 100 years after the death of Mayne, George Fox – founder of the Quakers – was also doing time in Launceston Castle. Fox was arrested in St Ives for distributing religious pamphlets. When he and his associates refused to pay their fines or to even remove their hats in court, they were jailed. Fox recorded the ordeal in his journal, describing the horrendous prison conditions in graphic detail. And many more years were to pass before religious freedom was enjoyed by all.

5

ELIZABETHAN

SAUCY SPANIARDS AND SALTY SEADOGS

THE ROYAL TREATMENT
Cornwall played a big part in the reign of Elizabeth I. Its location made it the English frontier in the war with Catholic Europe, as well as a starting gate in the race to colonise the New World and other parts of the globe.

And it was those two pursuits that primarily occupied the long reign of the Virgin Queen. However, it is partly thanks to a former Cornish resident that her reign was so long and successful for England. Elizabeth almost died of smallpox in 1562. The physician who supposedly saved her life was the German-born Burchard Kranich, better known as Dr Burcot. He had moved from Cornwall to London in the previous year to practise medicine. It is said Dr Burcot was the man who diagnosed the queen's smallpox. Despite being at first ridiculed for his diagnosis, the royal court successfully persuaded the physician (some historians say a dagger was required) to return and treat the queen when her condition became a threat to her life.

Queen Elizabeth I.

In saving the queen, Kranich, who ran a silver smelting house in the parish of St Veep, near Lostwithiel, before moving to the capital, could claim to have played his part in what became a golden age under the reign of Elizabeth: a time of international expansion and naval conquests, Cornwall at the forefront of much of it.

STAGE FRIGHT
Most will know that the Spanish failed in their bid to land on English soil in 1588. Devonian Sir Francis Drake – with the help of the weather – was successful in driving the Armada from British shores.

However, it is not so widely known that the Spanish *did* land in England – Cornwall to be precise – in the previous year, according to a rather fanciful tale.

It is said that Spanish soldiers came ashore at Penryn in 1587. However, they found very few people there. They became even more confused when they heard shouting from the other side of a hill. Unable to see who exactly was making the racket; the invaders assumed it was an army of a great number of men coming towards them. The Spanish made a hasty retreat and fled to their ships. The noise? Well, it was actually coming from an audience watching a performance of a Cornish play!

SPOT OF BOTHER

It was in Cornwall – on the Lizard peninsula – that the English first sighted the Spanish Armada in 1588. News of the arrival of the fleet of 130 ships was conveyed to London by a series of beacons that had been constructed all along the south coast of England for that very purpose.

It is said that the commander of the Armada had his eye on the Mount Edgcumbe estate, on the Cornish side of the Tamar, and had designated it for himself once the English were defeated.

The Spanish Armada.

Of course, the Spaniards were famously seen off – but they were to come back ...

IF AT FIRST YOU DON'T SUCCEED ...
The Spanish did *successfully* invade England in 1595 – at the invitation of a Cornishman. That is certainly one theory why the duchy suffered an incursion just a few years after the Spanish Armada failed in its bid.

Tristram Winslade wrote a letter to the King of Spain informing him that should the Spanish try again to land in England, they would find considerable support among the pro-Catholic Cornish people. Tristram was the grandson of John Winslade, who led the Cornish army during the Prayer Book Rebellion, a backlash against Protestantism.

Whether or not it was the letter that persuaded the Spanish to launch another attack on England will never be known, but attack they certainly did. In what is now known as the Battle of Cornwall, the Spanish set sail for Mount's Bay, landing first at Mousehole. It is said that every building in the village but for one was destroyed. A plaque records that Squire Jenkyn Keigwin was killed defending the only property to survive the ordeal. The invaders also ravaged the village of Paul.

The frightened residents of Mousehole and Paul fled to Newlyn and Penzance, but the Spanish did not spare these towns either. After making their point by holding a Catholic mass, the Spanish returned to their ships. Sir Francis Godolphin had tried to raise an army to see off the marauders, but it is said that he could only muster about a dozen men. Godolphin had feared this sort of attack. Just a couple of weeks earlier, he had written to Queen Elizabeth warning her of an imminent invasion, 'for the gathering of these Spaniards seemeth as a cloud that is like to fall shortly in some part of her Majesty's dominions'.

He probably should have guessed that the point of attack would be Mount's Bay, as there is an old Cornish prophecy concerning Merlin's Rock, which is situated at Mousehole:

'There shall land on the Rock of Merlin, Those who shall burn Paul, Penzance and Newlyn.' The Spanish had seemingly – and obligingly – fulfilled the prophecy.

Richard Carew, famous for *The Survey of Cornwall*, published in 1602, accused the Cornish of being cowards in not raising an army to fight the Spanish. Of course, if Tristram Winslade is anything to go by, they may have had their reasons for not doing so.

FIGHTING ON ALL FRONTS

Of the famous Elizabethan seafarers, Sir Richard Grenville probably lies closest to the hearts of the Cornish. The great mariner – cousin of Sir Walter Raleigh and friend of Sir Francis Drake – will forever be remembered for his gallant death in the Azores at the hands of the Spanish. Grenville, in charge of the *Revenge* – a ship once in the hands of Drake – was killed in 1591, but there is no doubt he went down fighting. He and his crew held off more than fifty Spanish galleons for hour after hour. Before Grenville and his men were defeated, they are thought to have taken, against all odds, the lives of hundreds of men, with a number of Spanish ships being destroyed in the process.

The Grenvilles of Stowe, near Bude, were an illustrious Cornish family. Although Richard Grenville was born at another of their homes – at Bideford in Devon – Stowe was the principal family seat from Medieval times. And though his many adventures took Grenville all over the globe, Cornwall remained a big part of his life. When not exploring some remote part of the world or defending the country from the threat of the Spanish Armada, Grenville spent some of his time 'fighting' specifically for the Cornish, as an MP and Sheriff of Cornwall.

It was not a surprise (or perhaps it was) that Grenville should become a sailor. His father, Roger, was captain of the *Mary Rose* and lost his life when that particular vessel – watched by Henry VIII – sank in the Solent.

'RALEIGH' ROUND

Sir Walter Raleigh – cousin of Sir Richard Grenville – also left his mark (or perhaps we should say 'scent') in Cornwall.

Like Grenville and Sir Francis Drake, Raleigh was born in Devon, but he held a number of administrative posts in the duchy. Antiquarian Richard Carew dedicated *The Survey of Cornwall* to Raleigh, who was serving as both Lord Warden of the Stannaries and Lord Lieutenant of Cornwall when the book was published in 1602. Many places claim Raleigh connections, including Padstow, where he reputedly had a home.

Raleigh was, of course, credited with bringing tobacco to England on return from one of his voyages, and it is said that he smoked his first tobacco in public while a guest of the Killigrews of Arwenack, which later became Falmouth. It was Raleigh who supposedly suggested to Sir John Killigrew that Arwenack would make an ideal port.

Both Raleigh and Drake served Cornwall in Parliament for spells. Raleigh was MP for Mitchell, while Drake was MP for Bossiney, near Tintagel. The Duke of Wellington – the man who defeated Napoleon at Waterloo – also served Mitchell in Parliament for a spell.

HER PIRATE

Not all of those who went to sea did so with honourable intentions. Many of the famous Elizabethan seafarers had their own motives for seeking out foreign vessels. And it is said that only thirty-four of the 226 ships that lined up for battle against the Spanish Armada in 1588 belonged to the navy. The rest were reputedly privateers.

Privateering was seen as more respectable than piracy, but, in many cases, there was not a lot of difference between the two occupations. Many English pirates simply used war as an excuse to carry out their sordid business.

Sir Francis Drake was a privateer and the Spanish were not the only ones to accuse him of piracy. Queen Elizabeth herself knew what he got up to and openly called him her pirate. He may have sailed under the flag of Elizabeth, but Drake was really – like most – out for himself. Of course, as long as he did his bit for queen and country at the same time, Elizabeth was happy with the arrangement. It is said that Drake hid some of his 'Spanish' treasures at Trematon Castle, near Saltash, and at one time his haul there amounted to some £20 million in today's money.

However, as relations with Spain worsened in the years preceding the Spanish Armada, Elizabeth had to attempt to stop the plundering and looting of Spanish ships, or at least try to satisfy the Spaniards that she was doing so. Needless to say, the Spanish were not at all convinced by her half-hearted attempts to halt Drake's private exploits, and relations between the two countries only deteriorated. Once war was declared with Spain, piracy against the Spanish did at least become legal.

Piracy off the Cornish coast had been a problem before Elizabeth came to the throne. However, the activity increased in the sixteenth century, continuing well into the next and beyond. Henry Every – often labelled the most successful English pirate in history – was a Devon man, like Drake, but he left a note towards the end of the seventeenth century to say that some of his treasure was buried in Cornwall – on the cliffs of the Lizard peninsula. It has never been found.

NOTHING TO REPORT
It was probably not a good idea to give Sir John Killigrew the job of ridding the Cornish coast of pirates – his family were the worst culprits!

The Killigrews of Arwenack, now Falmouth, were a powerful and influential family. As one of the leading Cornishmen, Sir John Killigrew was probably an obvious choice to lead the commission set up by Queen Elizabeth to examine the problem of piracy in his area, she now fearful of the declining relations with Spain that ultimately led to war.

However, one of the problems was that the Killigrews were part of that problem. When a Spanish ship was inadvertently driven into the harbour at Falmouth, it was boarded and looted, with reports that the crew were thrown overboard. It is said that no report from the commission followed the incident, simply because Killigrew did not call any commissioners to investigate it.

The Killigrews held much sway in Falmouth – they controlled the harbour – and, even if they were not involved in every treacherous act, they would certainly have known who was.

So many Killigrews – including the ladies – were involved in piracy, there is now much confusion surrounding their exploits, many members of the different generations being mistaken for another, with the result that it is difficult to provide a definitive account of their transgressions. And, of course, the true stories would no doubt have been embellished over the years. However, the Killigrews can certainly claim to be the leading Cornish pirates of all time.

HE SAW THE LIGHT

It is perhaps strange that a member of a family known for piracy should attempt to *stop* the looting of ships off the Cornish coast.

A later Sir John Killigrew applied for a patent to build a beacon or lighthouse at Lizard Point. There was much resistance to the idea. Wrecks could be – and locals often thought them to be – a godsend. Killigrew, in doing something to prevent shipwrecks, admitted: 'I take away God's grace from them (the locals).'

There were also fears that the light would increase the risk of invasion, helping to guide the enemy to Cornish shores. Pirates from North Africa were a big problem in the first half of the seventeenth century. Not content to attack English fishing fleets and traders in the Channel, many carried out raids on Cornish coastal communities, carrying off the locals to be used as slaves. Looe, in particular, suffered in this way, with a report that eighty inhabitants were seized by the marauding pirates in 1625.

Killigrew was granted a patent for his project in 1619, but had to fund it himself, and also ensure that the light was put out at the first sign of the approach of a foe. To keep the light in operation, Killigrew proposed that passing ships made a voluntary contribution. However, not enough income was generated in this way and the light went out until King James, alarmed by the increasing number of shipwrecks in the area, intervened and ordered that it be relit. However, when Killigrew died, the light went out again and The Lizard did not get another lighthouse until the mid-eighteenth century, though Killigrew can at least claim to have played his part in the beginning of lighthouses in England.

However, such was the reputation of the Killigrews; many have questioned the motives of this particular Sir John Killigrew. And there are even reports that the light was deliberately not lit if Killigrew had a reason not to light it. On one occasion, a ship was indeed wrecked off Lizard Point and Killigrew himself was accused of leading the salvage of the treasure, threatening death to any who interfered.

A HALT IN THE PILGRIMS' PROGRESS
No pirate or storm could stop the famous *Mayflower* from reaching the New World in 1620. The Pilgrims left English shores at Plymouth in Devon. However, it is reputed that Cornwall – and not Plymouth – was the *final* port of call for the brave travellers. Fearing their drinking water was contaminated – there had been an outbreak of cholera in Plymouth – the Pilgrims made an unscheduled stop at Newlyn to pick up a fresh supply. A plaque at Newlyn records this fact, though many dispute it and continue to claim Plymouth as the Pilgrims' final port of call. It is probably safe to say that Cornwall – whether the Pilgrims set foot on its soil or not – was, at the very least, the last place in England they ever saw.

6

CIVIL WAR AND RESTORATION

RIVALRY, REVELRY AND REVOLUTION

THANKS FOR YOUR HELP

For so long, England had been at war. However, by the mid-seventeenth century, it was not Catholic Europe that was the enemy. Now Englishmen – and Cornishmen – were fighting among themselves.

And Cornwall had a big part to play in the English Civil War. The doomed king himself – Charles I – found no greater ally than in the Cornish. Grateful for the support he received from the duchy, Charles wrote a letter of thanks in 1643 and ordered that it be displayed in every church and chapel throughout Cornwall so 'that as long as the history of these times and of this nation shall continue, the memory of how much that county hath merited from us and our crown, may be derived with it to posterity'.

WHOSE SIDE ARE YOU ON?

They like to do things differently in Cornwall, so it is perhaps no surprise that the Cornish bucked the trend in the West Country by supporting the Royalist cause

Cornwall
supported the
Royalists.

during the English Civil War. Most of the south-west of England, including neighbours Devon, supported the Parliamentarians.

However, there were good reasons for the Cornish to support the king. The independence of the county was at threat from the Parliamentarians. As a duchy, Cornwall was closely tied to the royal family, and its own Stannary Parliament afforded the Cornish certain rights and privileges. Most feared that the English Parliament would put an end to this independence and that Cornwall would lose its identity. The Parliamentarians were very 'English' and of a different culture. It must be remembered that many people in Cornwall did not even speak in the same tongue as the rest of the country. Royalist diarist Richard Symonds wrote in 1644: 'At Land's End they speak no English. All beyond Truro they speak the Cornish language.'

Religion also played a part in which side to take. Cornwall, a land of tradition, still celebrated its saints through holy days and feasts. The Protestant Parliamentarians did not approve of such things.

Indeed, the Royalist supporters were right to express these and many other fears. During the conflict, the Parliamentarians set fire to what became known as the Duchy Palace at Lostwithiel, home of the Stannary Parliament. Churches and shrines honouring Cornish saints – including holy wells – were also attacked.

Of course, not all in Cornwall supported the Royalists. A number of influential landowners, particularly in the east of the county, took the Parliamentarian side, though they were in the minority. In truth, most people did not want to take *any* side and were reluctant to get involved.

Charles I certainly appreciated the support he received from the people of Cornwall. In his famous letter of thanks to the county, he commented on the 'great and eminent courage and patience' of the Cornish people and 'their indefatigable prosecution of their great work against so potent an enemy'.

Of course, the Parliamentarians did not think so highly of the Cornish Royalists. A Parliamentarian pamphlet of the time declared that the men of Cornwall were 'very heathens, a corner of ignorants and atheists, drained from the mines'.

Like most things, how you viewed the world just depended on which side you were cheering for.

OH, BROTHER!

Choosing which side to support during the English Civil War was sometimes not an easy thing to do. Two Cornish brothers may have regretted their choices. Alexander and John Carew were both executed – one of them by the Parliamentarians and the other by the Royalists.

The siblings had started on the same side – the Carew family of Antony, near Saltash, were one of the few principal landowners of Cornwall to fight against the king. And John, for his pains, which included signing the death warrant of Charles I, was executed by the Royalists when the monarchy was restored in 1660. However, Sir Alexander had earlier suffered this same fate when he tried to betray his fellow Parliamentarians. In the early stages of the war, Plymouth was seized by Parliament's forces and Sir Alexander was put in command of the key defence of the town. As the Royalists started to fight back, including winning an important battle at Stratton in the north of Cornwall in 1643, Sir Alexander decided it was time to switch sides. He secretly contacted the Royalists and offered to surrender Plymouth in return for his life. However, a disloyal servant betrayed his master, and Sir Alexander was arrested and executed by his fellow Parliamentarians.

A BATTLE ROYAL

It may come as a surprise to learn that the man who led the Royalist cause in Cornwall during the English Civil War was, in fact, a Parliamentarian. Sir Bevil Grenville even played a part in bringing about the constitutional crisis that ultimately resulted in Englishmen taking up arms against each other.

However, even though Grenville originally sided with the Parliamentary opposition, by the outbreak of war, there was no stauncher supporter of the king. Indeed, Grenville became the focus of the Royalist cause in Cornwall. He was the first in the county to rally for the monarch and – with his death on the battlefield in 1643 – the Cornish Royalists were never the same again, at least in terms of a fighting force. Many were really fighting for the much-loved Grenville, rather than for a distant king. When their inspiration died in battle, many lost hope and interest in the war.

Sir Bevil Grenville had represented the Cornish people in Parliament from 1621. He was a friend and supporter of another influential Cornish MP, Sir John Eliot, and shared his views. Eliot fought vigorously for the rights of Parliament and was among those behind the Petition of Right, a document that Charles I was forced to accept and which, like the Magna Carta, saw the powers of the monarchy reduced. It was the resolutions of Eliot against illegal taxation that were being read in the House of Commons when the king ordered that Parliament be adjourned. Members of the House refused to comply and the speaker was held down until proceedings were concluded. As a result, Eliot and a number of his fellow rebel MPs were later arrested and Eliot died a prisoner in the Tower of London in 1632.

It is not known why Grenville switched his allegiance to the king. Most historians conclude that he simply believed that his fellow Parliamentarians had gone too far, and that he never wanted to see an end to the monarchy and the divine right of kings. Certainly, he served Charles I faithfully, and the king appreciated his efforts; in the pocket of Grenville – discovered following his death on the battlefield at Lansdowne, near Bath – was a treasured letter of thanks from Charles himself.

Grenville led the Cornish Royalists into three significant battles: two on home soil and his final one at Lansdowne. Although Grenville was a politician and no soldier, he did, however, possess fine leadership qualities, just like his grandfather – the explorer Sir Richard Grenville, who famously commanded the *Revenge*.

Sir Bevil, with Sir Ralph Hopton commanding the Royalist troops, first tasted victory at Braddock Down, near Liskeard, in January, 1643. The Parliamentarians, already with a foothold in neighbouring Devon, crossed the Tamar with the intention of winning Cornwall for Parliament. However, the invaders were routed close to Boconnoc, now famous for the house where William Pitt the Elder spent some of his childhood, it being built by his grandfather, Thomas, from the profits earned by bringing the world's largest diamond back from India.

Of those who survived the battle at Braddock Down, some 1,200 Roundheads were taken as prisoners and the others fled. Another Parliamentarian advance was halted in the north of Cornwall in May of the same year. The Battle of Stratton, near Bude, took place at what is now known as Stamford Hill just a couple of miles from Stowe, one of many homes belonging to the Grenvilles. The result was the same. The Parliamentarians were driven out of the county, even though the Royalists had fewer soldiers.

Hopton now had the initiative and headed east. The Cornish Royalists marched over the Tamar to fight another major battle, this time at Lansdowne. Sadly, for Bevil Grenville, it was to be his last. Despite helping the Royalists to another significant victory, Grenville was mortally wounded.

There were further victories for the Royalists, but the tide soon turned against them. The Parliamentarians had only temporarily been driven out of Cornwall – and they were to return. Fighting back under the command of the Earl of Essex, the Parliamentarians again crossed the Tamar in 1644. Despite reaching as far as Bodmin and torching what later became the Duchy Palace at Lostwithiel, they were again sent packing, suffering heavy defeats in and around Lostwithiel and Fowey. It was from the famous Castle Dore, north of Fowey, that Essex fled, leaving most of his army behind as he escaped to sea via a fishing boat. It is said that 7,000 Parliamentarians entered Cornwall, but only one-seventh escaped back across the border.

Of course, the Royalist celebrations did not last long. Nationally, the Parliamentarians were now on top. Writing in 1645, Sir Richard Grenville, brother of Sir Bevil, wrote: 'His Majesty hath no entire county in obedience but poor Cornwall.'

The Royalist army finally surrendered at Tresillian Bridge, near Truro. There were pockets of resistance – and things flared up again between 1648–51, notably in Penzance and the Helston area, where there were uprisings – but the war in Cornwall was effectively over.

ONE 'KNIGHT' STAND

Royalist supporter Sir John Arundell was left holding the fort. While the English Civil War was over for most in Cornwall by 1646, it was only really just beginning for him.

Arundell, of Trerice, near Newquay, was already past retirement age when Charles I gave him command of Pendennis Castle. The Royalists were a spent force and the king's days were numbered, but Arundell was made of stern stuff and was willing to fight until the bitter end.

Queen Henrietta Maria, wife of the king, sheltered at Pendennis before fleeing to France, while her son, who later became Charles II, also took refuge within the castle walls from the pursuing Parliamentarian Thomas Fairfax, before escaping to the Isles of Scilly.

Fairfax arrived at Falmouth in the spring of 1646 and sent word to Arundell demanding the surrender of Pendennis. However, Arundell made it clear that he had no intention of throwing in the towel. He replied: 'I resolve that I will here bury myself before I deliver up this castle to such as fight against his Majesty.'

·Fairfax chose not to storm the castle. Not for the first time during the war, he decided to sit tight. There was no escape route for those within the castle walls and Fairfax starved them out. However, he did not count on the resolve of the 'prisoners' inside. The siege lasted some five months. The garrison eventually ran out of supplies – the Royalist supporters forced to eat horses – but only when there was nothing left did they finally surrender. The starving survivors triumphantly marched out of the castle with trumpets sounding and drums beating. Pendennis was one of the last Royalist strongholds in England to fall.

As for Arundell, his punishment included the confiscation of property – the Arundells of Trerice were major landowners – but his life was spared. Sadly, he died before the Restoration, when the monarchy was returned to the throne.

DID YOU HAVE A GOOD DAY, DEAR?

The day 30 January 1649 was not a good one for Charles I. Not only was he executed at the hands of the Parliamentarians on this day, but his personal belongings were lost at sea. A ship called *Garland* was transporting most of his property to France when it was wrecked off Godrevy, near St Ives. Most on board perished. On the bright side, at least the unfortunate king no longer had any need for the clothes he lost!

RESTORATION REWARDS

The Cornish gained a lot of friends because of their efforts during the English Civil War. Historian Thomas Fuller, in *The History of the Worthies of England*, remarked that the loyalty shown by the people towards the monarchy had done much to change the view people had of the county. He said: 'It must be pitied that these people [the Cornish], misguided by their leaders, have so often abused their valour in rebellions ...' However, he added that they 'have since

Charles II.

plentifully repaired their credit, by their exemplary valour and loyalty in our late civil wars'.

It is said that it took a while for Charles II to remember just what the Cornish Royalists did for him and his family. Amid the joyful celebrations at the Restoration in 1660 – when the Stuarts were returned to the throne – the rewards were slow in coming. The fun-loving Charles, preoccupied by many state affairs (and parties), needed to be reminded of the debt he owed to his duchy supporters.

And the Cornish were owed a lot. There is a fanciful story that a Cornishman even took a bullet meant for Charles I, not that he intended to. The king – who spent much time in Cornwall during the troubles – was staying at Hall Manor, Bodinnick, in 1644, when a ball from a musket fired on the other side of the river at Fowey whizzed past him and hit a fisherman.

Sir Richard Grenville, like brother Sir Bevil, also died before the Restoration, but he did gain the reward of being immortalised in fiction – in the Daphne du Maurier novel *The King's General*.

One Grenville (though he changed the family name to Granville) who did live to be rewarded was John, the son and heir of Sir Bevil. John – who became Earl of Bath – played a major role in bringing about the return of the monarchy and received many other titles for his efforts.

The most unusual reward was handed out to Thomas Killigrew, who had followed Prince Charles into exile and returned with him at the Restoration, when Charles became king. Killigrew, who wrote bawdy comedies, was, alongside Sir William Davenant, granted the monopoly of the London theatres at their reopening. Killigrew formed the King's Company and built the first Drury Lane playhouse. He revived some of William Shakespeare's almost forgotten plays.

It was not just individuals who were honoured. Charles II elevated Penzance to the status of a coinage town for the tin industry because of its show of support for the monarchy in 1648. The killing of dozens of rebel Royalists in the town prompted hundreds of Cornishmen to pick up arms again, but the rebellion ended in another victory for the Parliamentarians.

It was not until Charles I was executed in 1649 that Cornwall was finally forced to submit to Oliver Cromwell and it was a further two years before Cornish resistance was broken with the capture of the Isles of Scilly, the last Royalist outpost.

Of course, some Parliamentarians were also 'rewarded' at the Restoration for the role they played. Fowey-born Hugh Peter, leading chaplain of Cromwell, was among those executed. One individual honoured at the Restoration who should not be overlooked – and that might be difficult to do anyway – is a certain Anthony Payne.

NO 'PAYNE', NO GAIN

There was no bigger hero of the English Civil War in Cornwall than Anthony Payne – literally. Payne stood at more than 7ft tall. His exact height has been much debated and 7ft 4in appears to be the maximum any historian has dared to suggest.

Charles II recognised the loyalty and courage Payne displayed in serving Sir Bevil Grenville, the Royalist leader in Cornwall during the hostilities. The restored king appointed Payne as Halberdier of the Guns at Plymouth Citadel after reclaiming the throne in 1660. He also commissioned a painting of Payne that was as big as the man himself!

Payne, all 38 stone of him, faithfully followed Grenville in battle and, because of his strength, would have been a useful ally. After his master fell at Lansdowne, Payne is said to have carried the body back to the Stowe family home for burial at Kilkhampton.

When Payne himself died, his Stratton home – now the *Tree Inn* – had to be reconstructed in order to get the coffin in and out.

BLOOD PRESSURE

Religion and politics continued to divide the nation, long after the English Civil War had ended and the monarchy had been restored. People rose and fell, often because of their beliefs and views.

One man who lived during these unsettling times was Cornish physician Richard Lower. It was not enough that he was the most noted medical man in London – he still fell from grace when the throne of England changed hands.

Lower, who was born at St Tudy, near Bodmin, is remembered for his pioneering work in medical science. In the mid 1660s, he became the first man to perform a transfusion of blood from one dog to another, which led to the same operation being performed on a human.

Lower was physician to Charles II and faithfully tended to the monarch during his final illness. However, following the death of the king in 1685; Lower lost his position in the royal court because of his anti-Catholic views, with the new monarch – James II – a supporter of Rome. Lower fell from favour and his medical practice suffered as a result, the physician eventually retiring to Cornwall.

TRELAWN-WHO?
Most people in Cornwall know the name. You will find numerous streets within the county that have adopted it and thousands even sing it at the top of their voices during rugby matches. Indeed, the name 'Trelawny' is a household one within the duchy.

But – it has to be said – many do not have a clue as to the reason why. Even if they state correctly that Sir Jonathan Trelawny was a bishop, that is often all they can say about the man who has given his name to what has now become the unofficial anthem of Cornwall itself.

The Cornish Victorian author Robert Stephen Hawker was responsible for immortalising Bishop Trelawny in song more than 130 years after the clergyman was imprisoned in the Tower of London. It is thought that Hawker's ballad *The Song of the Western Men* – sometimes just called *Trelawny* – is a modern version of a folk song. However, some argue that Hawker was wrong to assume that the Trelawny in the original song referred to Bishop Trelawny and suggest that it actually referred to his grandfather, a Royalist leader who was imprisoned by the Parliamentarians prior to the English Civil War. There are other theories as well.

Jonathan Lord Bishopp of Bristol.
Printed and sold by John Overton at the white horse without Newgate.

Bishop Trelawny.

However, Bishop Trelawny – whether or not it was meant for him – is probably deserving of becoming the subject of a patriotic anthem.

Bishop Jonathan Trelawny was born in the parish of Pelynt, near Looe, in 1650, the son of a Cornish baronet. He was still only in his mid thirties when James II appointed him Bishop of Bristol very soon after coming to the throne. James was a Catholic and believed he would earn the support of Trelawny, who came from a family of staunch Royalists. He was wrong.

Trelawny became one of seven bishops who refused to accept the king's Declaration of Indulgence, which granted religious toleration to Catholics and other dissenters.

The bishops argued that the king had no legal right to change the law. Not surprisingly, James was furious and had all seven bishops imprisoned in the Tower.

'And shall Trelawny live? Or shall Trelawny die?' Hawker wrote.

Trelawny lived. The king lost the subsequent trial, the court siding with the rebel bishops. It meant that 20,000 Cornishmen were not required to march to London in support of the bishop, as the song implies they were preparing to do, the bishop being acquitted in triumph, amid much celebration in his home county.

James took his case to Parliament, but lost again. England was making it clear it did not want a Catholic king – and a Protestant revolution was now on the horizon.

Trelawny himself took the oath of allegiance to the Protestant William of Orange and, in 1688, James fled the throne.

Bishop Trelawny was a determined individual who would go to great lengths to get his way. Of all the seven bishops – who included the Archbishop of Canterbury – James referred to him as 'the most-saucy' of the lot.

Today, Hawker's patriotic song is most often heard when Cornwall are playing rugby, the fans themselves now known as 'Trelawny's Army'.

'And shall Trelawny live?' Yes, he shall – at least in Cornwall – even if many need a little reminder as to exactly who he was.

A 'UNION' MAN WHO TOED THE LINE

The people of Cornwall have long fought for their independence, so it is therefore ironic that a Cornishman should be responsible for the most famous *union* in British history – the very one that created 'Great Britain'.

However, the remarkable Sir Sidney Godolphin was probably the perfect man for arranging the Acts of Union between England and Scotland in 1707. It appears that

Godolphin had a knack of getting on with almost everyone. His skills of diplomacy would have been put to good use during his forty-plus years as a leading statesman.

As monarchs came and went during troubled times, Godolphin stayed and prospered, holding some of the highest offices of state. In fact, Godolphin is probably unique in British politics for gaining the trust of no fewer than four consecutive sovereigns, often earning him the accolade of being called the greatest statesman to have served the country. On his death, the Duchess of Marlborough declared him 'the best man that ever lived'.

Godolphin was born on the Godolphin estate, near Helston. He first came to prominence during the reign of Charles II following the Restoration. His early roles included diplomatic missions to Spain and France, and he fast earned a reputation for being good with money, the nation's finances eventually trusted to him when he became First Lord of the Treasury.

Godolphin became the most trusted minister of Catholic sympathiser James II, but still found favour when the Protestant William of Orange replaced him on the throne following the 'Glorious Revolution' of 1688. Godolphin even managed to correspond with the fallen monarch at the same time as serving the new one. It was a dangerous game to play, but Godolphin was good at playing it.

It was while serving Queen Anne that Godolphin successfully negotiated the Acts of Union between England and Scotland. That union removed the threat of Scotland siding with France or any other rival. There was also the fear that the Scots would attempt to bring back the Catholic Stuarts by making James II's son (the 'Old Pretender') their king at the death of Anne. The union proved a success and the new 'country' did indeed become 'great'.

Godolphin was a non-party man, a go-between for the Crown and Parliament. The fact that monarchs (Protestant or Catholic) were prepared to overlook his previous allegiances highlight the high regard in which he was held. His expertise in finance opened doors that would have been shut for others.

Today, the name 'Godolphin' is, of course, perhaps better known in horseracing circles, the family being responsible for bringing the Arabian horse to England. Sidney Godolphin himself loved racing and gambling, and he certainly sits among the thoroughbreds of British politics.

IT'S NO GOOD 'PRETENDING'

Those wishing to put the Catholic House of Stuart back on the throne could not be blamed for thinking that Cornwall might be able to help achieve that aim; the county was home to many influential Jacobite supporters.

And that is why it was targeted to play a key role in the Jacobite rising of 1715. However, its leaders – including Sir Richard Vyvyan of Trelowarren House on the Lizard peninsula – were arrested before it took off in the way that had been hoped. James Paynter, of Trekenning, did not give up and, famously, in the market square at St Columb Major, proclaimed the 'Old Pretender' (James Francis Edward Stuart). The uprising was quashed, and Paynter and his fellow rebels fled to London. They were eventually captured and imprisoned to await trial for high treason. Paynter was tried at Launceston and acquitted. The fact his acquittal sparked widespread celebrations throughout Cornwall only emphasised the fact that the county was in sympathy with the Jacobites, and vindicated the original plan to kick-start the rising in the West Country. The Jacobite strongholds were mainly concentrated in Scotland, Ireland and Northern England. However, Wales and the south-west of England, particularly Cornwall, had a significant support for the movement that sought to return a Catholic Stuart to the throne.

The Paynter family was so associated with the Jacobites that it was also later wrongly accused of harbouring the

'Young Pretender' (Charles Edward Stuart) after the 1745 Jacobite rising.

HE KEPT THEM POSTED

To suggest that entrepreneur Ralph Allen might not have become the man he did if he had not detected a Jacobite plot is perhaps doing him a disservice.

Many claim that his career took off when he became the protégé of none less than General George Wade, the constant thorn in the side of the Jacobites. Allen was rewarded with a patronage from Wade for his part in preventing another uprising. However, even though the support of Wade would not have done him any harm, it is probably safe to say that Allen was the type of man that would have made it to the top with or without any help.

What Cornish-born Allen exactly did to thwart the Jacobites and earn the backing of Wade has been much debated. Certainly, as postmaster at Bath, he would have been in a good position to intercept any written communication between the rebel Jacobites. However, Cornish scholar Henry Jenner suggested that Allen was, in fact, the man responsible for the arrest of James Paynter, the rebel who led the failed uprising in St Columb Major. Jenner, a later resident of St Columb Major and famous for his attempts to revive the Cornish language, said that Allen was at the post office in St Columb Major, and not Bath, when he became suspicious of some of the goings-on there. It is said that the servant of Paynter, who was in hiding in London with his master following the 1715 uprising, was in the habit of corresponding with a lover in St Columb Major. According to Jenner, Allen opened one of the letters, suspecting that it had been written by one of the suspects on the run. He informed the authorities and Paynter was eventually arrested. The post office at St Columb Major was run by Allen's grandmother and he had helped her out in his younger days. In fact, it was there that he had caught the eye. He was given an official job in the service, eventually being elevated to postmaster at Bath, becoming the youngest man in the country – then 19 – to hold such a position. Even though Allen was working in Bath by 1715, his connections with St Columb Major could support the theory of Jenner.

Allen made his fortune when he introduced the first cross-country postal system. He could not understand why mail from Bath to a location in the north of England had to go via London. The government agreed to farm out all the cross-country posts in England and Wales. With the financial aid of Wade, Allen bought the franchise and became very rich.

Full of enterprise, Allen did not rest on his laurels. He bought some quarries near Bath and the honey-coloured stone produced at Combe Down was used to construct some of the city's iconic buildings. It is said that Allen – who served Bath as mayor for a period – was so successful, he almost ended up running the city. He was treated like a celebrity and acted like one. He built his own palace – Prior Park – and put a statue of Wade at its entrance. Royalty, politicians and writers were among the distinguished guests. Henry Fielding, one of them, modelled Squire Allworthy in *Tom Jones* on this celebrated Cornishman who became one of the most influential and famous figures of his time.

CRUNCH TIME

Another enterprising Cornishman also left his mark in Bath at the same time as Ralph Allen. In fact, it was Allen who introduced William Oliver to Bath society.

Oliver, who was born at Ludgvan, near Penzance, served as a physician at what became the Royal Mineral Water Hospital. There he invented the famous Bath Oliver biscuit. It followed his Bath bun, the biscuit deemed to be a less fattening alternative for his patients!

7

THE SEA

SMUGGLERS, SHIPWRECKS AND SAILORS

RELIEVE THEM OF THEIR DUTIES

Cornwall and smuggling – the two go hand in hand. No other county in England is so linked to the trade. After all, you are never far from the sea in Cornwall.

Indeed, you will find museums devoted to the history of smuggling; pubs that still point out where goods were hidden and gravestones reminding us that it was no romantic occupation, but a sometimes brutal and dangerous one.

Smuggling in Cornwall peaked in the mid-eighteenth century, though it had been going on long before that. It is difficult to put a date on when it all started. Of course, wherever you find a tax, you will find people unwilling to pay it. The tinners were smuggling tin out of Cornwall for that reason back in the Middle Ages. At some point, the smuggling of imported goods turned from isolated moments of opportunity into a major industry. Some suggest the turning point came at the end of the seventeenth century when a tax on imported salt was introduced. In Cornwall, salt from the Continent was used for curing pilchards. It was a

Smugglers were from all walks of life.

big industry and no surprise that many sought to cut their costs. It is not difficult to imagine a few tea bags and the odd bottle of brandy being placed in the undeclared cargoes of salt at the same time.

High import duties often doubled the price of some goods. As more and more took to smuggling, the taxes increased, with the result that more and more entered the 'game'. For a spell in the second half of the eighteenth century, it is said that 470,000 gallons of brandy and 350,000lb of tea were being smuggled into the county every year.

One has to remember that there was much poverty in Cornwall. For many, smuggling became a necessity. However, smuggling was not confined to the peasant. Many wealthy landowners got involved too. In fact, almost every-one was at it. John Wesley, founder of Methodism, wrote on a visit to St Ives: 'I found an accursed thing among them; well-nigh one and all bought or sold uncustomed goods.'

NEVER ON A SUNDAY

John Carter was Cornwall's most notorious smuggler – at least for six days of the week. That was because Carter – better known as the 'King of Prussia' – was also a religious man and is said to have refused to work on a Sunday.

Carter considered himself to be a man of honour. On one occasion, customs officers raided his house in his absence, seizing goods that Carter had only recently landed. Carter was due to deliver those goods to a customer and feared his business integrity would be at stake should he not do so. Even though he may have had a good excuse for not fulfilling his side of the bargain, Carter decided to do something about it. He broke into the customs house at Penzance and got his contraband back. It appears he got away with the crime through lack of evidence, but it is said that the customs officers had no doubt that he was responsible, as the only goods taken were the ones that they had earlier seized from Carter himself. The thief had not touched contraband confiscated from other sources. It is said that Carter – being an 'honest' man – did not want to take anything that did not belong to him!

The life of Carter may have been a paradox, but he would not have been the only smuggler to turn up at church on Sunday mornings. Most people genuinely believed that smuggling was a fair trade and that they were not doing anything wrong, the extortionate taxes being adequate justification. There are even tales of members of the clergy allowing smugglers to store contraband in the church vestry, or themselves holding a lantern on the beach as the boats were being unloaded.

The Carters were devout Methodists, but all were engaged in the trade. However, Harry Carter – brother of John – was stirred by his conscience and eventually gave up smuggling ... for preaching.

John Carter is said to have acquired his nickname from his childhood, when he insisted on being his hero Frederick the Great – the King of Prussia – when playing soldiers with his brothers. The name stuck. Indeed, the spot where the Carters carried out their business – situated between Penzance and Porthleven – is now known as Prussia Cove.

IF YOU CAN'T BEAT THEM …

There were too few customs officers to stop the flourishing smuggling trade in the eighteenth century, and it could not have helped when those supposed to be on your side were at it as well.

John Knill was a collector of customs at St Ives for some twenty years, but that did not stop him profiting from the illegal trade at the same time. He managed to combine a successful smuggling career with his day job. Knill was a leading citizen and even served the town as mayor for a spell. It was he that built the obelisk that still overlooks St Ives Bay, intending it to be his mausoleum, even though he was eventually buried in London.

Knill cut a figure of respectability and goodness. And you could just imagine the praise he must have received for fitting out, at his own expense, a privateer during the French wars. However, instead of seeking out the enemy, it is said it was secretly put to use as a smuggling vessel.

Knill was also linked to a boat loaded with smuggled china that ran aground in the area. It is reputed that the faithful crew, on making their escape from the stricken vessel, made a point of removing the ship's papers in order not to implicate who was really behind the operation. Even the investigating customs officer – not Knill on this occasion – is said to have helped himself to some of the cargo, though the story goes that a local noticed his bulging clothes and ensured his haul became worthless with a couple of well-aimed strikes from his stick!

Polperro, near Looe, was a hotbed of smuggling and one former resident certainly knew how to cash in. Zephaniah Job was known as 'the smugglers' banker'. He was so respected in the village that the free traders (the Cornish preferred to call smuggling free trading) trusted him with their finances. He even issued his own banknotes. As well as maintaining the accounts of the villagers, Job would finance their various smuggling ventures.

PUT THAT IN YOUR PIPE AND SMOKE IT

Evidence of the smuggling era can be found in many places in Cornwall, none more so than in Falmouth.

Next to the customs house – where revenue was collected from legally imported goods – is a brick furnace, known as the King's Pipe. It was used to burn contraband tobacco, or at least that which did not find its way into the pockets of corrupt customs officers!

LOOK WHAT THE STORM BLEW IN

Cornwall was not short of smugglers, wreckers and pirates. However, Cruel Coppinger was all three of those ... and worse! That is, if we are to believe Victorian writer Robert Stephen Hawker, who did his bit to immortalise this semi-legendary scoundrel who terrorised the north Cornwall coast.

No doubt, the durability of the legend of Coppinger owes much to the vivid imagination of Hawker, who, in sharing the story with the rest of the country, may have been a little liberal with the truth.

Hawker informs us that Coppinger arrived at Welcombe on the border with Devon during a storm, as all villains should! The locals were out in force. 'The shore and the heights were dotted with watchers for wreck,' Hawker wrote. They spotted a foreign rig doing battle with the gigantic waves. The skipper – 'one man of Herculean height and mould' – jumped from the doomed ship and swam to shore. Before the eyes of the stunned locals, he grabbed one of their horses and galloped away, the animal heading for its home – that also being the abode of Dinah Hamlyn. Hawker tells us that Coppinger installed himself at her home and, when her father died, he married her.

And that was really the beginning, as Hawker penned: 'His evil nature, so long smouldering, broke out like a wild beast uncaged. All at once the house became the den and refuge of every lawless character on the coast.'

The reputation of Coppinger and his gang grew, and he was accused of all sorts of hideous crimes, to the point that the law were too scared to even venture out to this wild and remote part of Cornwall. However, it appears things did get a little bit too hot for even Coppinger in the end and he eventually fled – going the same way as he had come and, needless to say, making his escape during another storm!

WHEN THE SHIP COMES IN
Cornwall is synonymous with wrecking, and there are many tales of ships being deliberately lured to destruction. But, in reality, there was not really a need for intervention – there were enough 'natural' shipwrecks. The Cornish coast is so treacherous; more often than not, vessels would come a cropper on stormy nights without the need for anyone to try to confuse mariners by waving 'false' lights.

In fact, Cornwall has become the 'graveyard' of more ships than any other county in England, and many people – if not responsible for the actual wrecking of a ship – certainly believed that they were entitled to the spoils of a doomed vessel. The famous Quaker, George Fox, wrote in 1659: 'It was the custom of that country [Cornwall], at such a time, both rich and poor went out to get as much of the wreck as they could, not caring to save the people's lives; and in some parts of the country they called shipwrecks God's grace.'

In 1753, the government strengthened the law against wrecking, making stealing from a shipwreck punishable by death. Cornishman William Pearse, a pensioner from St Gennys, near Bude, was the first to fall foul of the new act. He was executed at Launceston in 1767.

One of the worst naval disasters in British history involved a fleet of vessels that went down off the Isles of

Scilly in 1707 with the loss of up to 2,000 lives. It has been suggested that the commander of the fleet, Sir Cloudesley Shovell, was washed up on the beach alive, only to be murdered by a local woman intent on securing his emerald ring. Even if many people would not go this far, the majority, it is probably fair to say, would have probably tried harder to salvage the cargo than the crew.

HE DIDN'T DESERT A SINKING SHIP

In a remote church on the windswept north Cornwall coast is a physical reminder that many ships did not make it home. The figurehead of the *Caledonia* – one of those ill-fated vessels – was brought ashore by the vicar of Morwenstow, none other than the Rev. Robert Stephen Hawker, a man whose name is now used to describe this whole area of Cornwall; such was his influence and renown.

But the church at Morwenstow in 'Hawker Country' contains more than a relic of a doomed ship. In the churchyard, beneath what is now a replica figurehead (the original is now inside the church), lie the bodies of the crew itself. Of course, you would expect bodies in a churchyard, but usually salvagers of shipwrecks only had eyes for the treasures washed up on their beaches, not the corpses. In general, most victims – if their bodies were recovered at all – were buried in communal pits with little or no ceremony. Hawker was a man of compassion. He made it his mission to give these unknown sailors a Christian burial and would go to great lengths to retrieve their remains. It is believed some forty or fifty mariners are buried in the churchyard at Morwenstow. There was just one survivor from the *Caledonia* when it perished in the early 1840s. Hawker gave him a home for six weeks and also set about locating the bodies of his fellow crewmen.

Hawker became famous for his devotion to burying the victims of shipwrecks. He would often sit on the cliffs – in a small hut that he constructed from driftwood and which still stands today – looking out to sea, fearing that

Robert Stephen Hawker.

any change in the weather might bring another hapless ship closer to its doom. Hawker once wrote: 'I hear in every gust of the gale a dying sailor's cry.'

And he had good reason to pen those words. This part of the coastline was one of the worst in the country for shipwrecks. Some eighty wrecks were recorded in the Bude area in the years 1824–74, a period that covered Hawker's four-decade incumbency at Morwenstow.

Hawker is remembered today for many things: his writing and for being the instigator of the Harvest Festival among them. However, most will think of his eccentricities: his unusual attire ... smoking opium ... cats and dogs accompanying him to church.

It is no wonder this unconventional clergyman became one of the best-known clerics in England. The names of those sailors he pulled from the sea have not lived so long in the memory, but at least, thanks to Hawker, those unfortunate individuals have not been totally forgotten.

Devon clergyman and writer Sabine Baring-Gould, along with penning famous hymns, produced a biography of Hawker. As a folklorist, he was also fascinated with tales of wrecking and wrote much on the subject.

I'VE GOT THAT SINKING FEELING AGAIN

They say that lightning doesn't strike twice. Well, it did in Cornwall on 22 January 1809. There were at least two shipwrecks on that day – at the same place.

HMS *Primrose*, sailing for Spain, was the first to succumb to the deadly Manacles, treacherous rocks off the coast of The Lizard. It is believed there was just one survivor from the crew of more than 100.

On that same day, the transport ship *Dispatch* suffered the same fate. It was carrying soldiers, this time returning home from Spain after doing battle in the Peninsula War. Once again, dozens perished, with just a few survivors.

LULL BEFORE THE STORM

In 1803 the *Royal Cornwall Gazette* announced that Lloyd's had 'liberally contributed' the sum of £50 towards the purchase of a lifeboat for Mount's Bay. It added that the total cost of the vessel would be £150, which the 'inhabitants thereof, and of Cornwall in general, are requested to contribute towards carrying this laudable undertaking into effect'. And so the first lifeboat station in Cornwall was established at Penzance.

The newspaper article reminded readers of the many wrecks – and loss of life – that had occurred in Mount's Bay the previous winter.

Needless to say, most were expecting the new ten-oar lifeboat to be put to good use. It was not. Perhaps we should count our blessings as there was no one to rescue, but the Penzance lifeboat did not perform even one service in nine years. And, in 1812, it was sold for just 20 guineas.

The lifeboat service got off to a slow start in Cornwall.

Of course, a station for Mount's Bay was re-established and more lifeboat stations added throughout Cornwall in the 1820s after Sir William Hillary had formed the National Institution for the Preservation of Life from Shipwreck (which later became the RNLI). However, Cornwall and Devon still only had a dozen lifeboats between them in the mid-nineteenth century.

It is a good job that Cornwall was eventually to get a few more. Its coastline is the most treacherous in Britain. Since the High Middle Ages, some 6,000 vessels have been wrecked off its shores.

ROCKET SCIENCE SAVED LIVES

What price do you put on a life? Not a very high one if the 'gratitude' shown to inventor Henry Trengrouse is anything to go by.

Thousands of lives at sea have been saved because of his work and yet his financial reward was pitiful. He died almost destitute and largely unappreciated. In fact, it is only really in recent times that he has started to get the recognition he deserves.

Trengrouse, who lived all his life in Helston, is credited as being the inventor of the rocket lifesaving apparatus, an early form of the breeches buoy – the rope-based rescue device used to remove people from stricken vessels.

Trengrouse set about helping those in trouble at sea after witnessing the demise of the frigate HMS *Anson* in 1807. The vessel was driven on to rocks off Loe Bar during a storm. Horrified onlookers watched as people were forced to swim for their lives. More than 100 people died.

Trengrouse spent every spare penny trying to come up with something that would have helped those aboard HMS *Anson*. He had no financial help in devising his rocket and line that could be fired from the shore to a vessel at sea. Trengrouse came up with his design very soon after the HMS *Anson* tragedy, but it took him many years to earn the approval of those who mattered. Finally, in 1818, Trengrouse got the thumbs up from the Admiralty and Trinity House. The latter organisation went as far as to suggest that no ship should be without rocket lifesaving apparatus. However, the government ordered just twenty sets, preferring to have them constructed 'in house'. They paid Trengrouse £50 compensation. The Society of Arts awarded Trengrouse 30 guineas and a silver medal for his efforts. However, it appears his endeavours were a little more appreciated overseas: Alexander I of Russia congratulated him on his achievement, enclosing a diamond ring with his letter. Sadly, Trengrouse was later forced to sell it in order to support his family; his ongoing attempts to perfect his apparatus leaving him penniless.

KEEP WATCHING

Few doubt what a grand job the RNLI does; however, much of its work goes unseen with most rescues occurring way out at sea. That is why one rescue off the Cornish coast is perhaps remembered above all others.

Indeed, there were not just one or two to witness the rescue of the Sandersons after their vessel foundered off Cape Cornwall – but an estimated 6,000! And those who lined the shore to watch the drama unfold at the beginning of 1851 had plenty of time to contemplate just how tough saving lives can be – the rescue taking two whole days.

The *New Commercial* struck rocks – known as The Brisons – during a terrific storm. No one witnessed the ship break into pieces, but a coastguard spotted the survivors the next morning, the rocks being only a mile or so from the coastline. One crew member did manage to get ashore, but the others – apart from the Sandersons who were left stranded on the rocks – all drowned.

Despite the couple being within sight of the growing number of onlookers lining the clifftop, the rescue boats failed in their numerous attempts to get to them due to the stormy conditions. Finally, a rocket line fired from a rescue vessel did reach the pair. Mrs Sanderson was the first to be pulled through the water to safety, then her husband. Captain Sanderson survived the ordeal, but Mrs Sanderson died from exhaustion and exposure before the rescue boat reached the shore. She was buried in the churchyard at Sennen.

The greatest number of people rescued in one single operation by the RNLI took place in Cornwall, off Lizard Point, in 1907. Not one life was lost – all 450-plus people on board *Suevic* safely brought ashore.

Tragically, on the flip side, there are sometimes no survivors, as highlighted by the infamous Penlee lifeboat disaster of 1981. In their bid to rescue the eight crew members of the *Union Star*, the eight volunteer lifeboatmen of the *Solomon Browne* also perished with them.

OLD DREADNOUGHT HAD NEW IDEAS

The mid-eighteenth century was a golden era for Britain at sea, and a Cornishman might have earned the honour of being its greatest maritime hero if a certain Lord Nelson had not come along.

Admiral Edward Boscawen – aka 'Old Dreadnought' – won the hearts of the nation and comfortably sits among the greatest of British admirals.

Like Nelson, Boscawen, who was born at Tregothnan, in the village of St Michael Penkevil, near Truro, proved his worth in times of war. However, he also gained his place in maritime history for showing a side of his character so often missing in great leaders: compassion.

Few admirals had much – if any – regard for their crew. Most low-ranking sailors were viewed as being replaceable. While the high-ranking officers were afforded some comforts aboard ship, the lowest lived in dreadful conditions. Boscawen did much to change that. He set about

improving hygiene on ships by fitting ventilators, in the
hope that cleaner air below deck would help alleviate sickness. Boscawen also tried to offer his men a better diet. On
one occasion while stationed off Brest to keep an eye on
the French fleet, he gave his men the task of cultivating an
unoccupied island. Not only did it relieve their boredom,
but also provided fresh food for the larder, a luxury few
ships at sea would have enjoyed. Of course, it is difficult to
prove that those who served Boscawen were healthier, but
many sea captains adopted his innovations in the hope of
emulating his success.

Boscawen won many battles for Britain and was respected
by all. He gained his affectionate nickname while serving
HMS *Dreadnought*, the idea being that he was almost the
ship himself, and that it would have been nothing without
him in charge of it.

Boscawen joined the navy as a boy and was a captain
by the time he reached his mid twenties. Despite his caring
attitude, he was no pushover. When he discovered liquor
hidden away in the cabins of his officers on one occasion,
he threw it overboard and reputedly never allowed another
drop of alcohol aboard his ships again.

Old Dreadnought – the name stayed with him long after
his association with that ship ended – led a life of service.
He was also a politician, becoming MP for Truro from
1742 until his death in 1761. Indeed, he never stopped
thinking about the people of Cornwall and did all he could
to help them.

'ADMIRAL' EFFORTS FOR THE CORNISH

You would expect Cornwall to produce its fair share of
mariners. With the sea playing such an important part in
the lives of Cornish residents, it is not surprising that many
sought a career on the ocean waves.

However, it appears that Cornwall might have produced
more than its fair share of sailors; some people certainly
thought so. Many were of the opinion that Admiral

Edward Boscawen gave too much preference to Cornish officers, and cheekily nicknamed Britain's sea force the 'Cornish' Navy.

Certainly, Boscawen – though helping every sailor through his attempts to improve their working conditions – did believe in the adage: charity begins at home. When he needed new recruits, he would often look no further than Cornwall. He was well aware that there was much poverty in the duchy. On one occasion, he signed up fifty men from Penzance and even advanced their wages to help the families they were to leave behind.

The generosity of Boscawen to his fellow kinsmen was so great, it could not go without comment in the House of Commons following his death in 1761, which was described as 'an event that greatly affects this country, there being a vast number of Cornishmen whose bread, and hopes of preferment depended entirely on him'.

Social reformer Elizabeth Montagu, leader of the Blue Stockings Society, writing more than five years earlier, also pointed out the popularity of Boscawen:

> In these days of discontent, all are pleased with him, and I assure you it will discredit any new administration if he is excluded his share in it. No! That cannot, shall not be; it would put the very ocean in a storm, and the large continent of Cornwall into a rebellion.

MEDITERRANEAN MEN

Sea commanders William Bligh and Sir Charles Penrose were peers who belonged to quite different schools.

While Bligh – of *Bounty* fame – belonged to the old school, being a tough and uncompromising disciplinarian, Penrose was a disciple of Admiral Edward Boscawen and had his feet firmly in the camp that believed in treating all sailors as human beings.

Penryn-born Penrose, like Boscawen, enjoyed a productive career at sea, almost twenty-five years of it coinciding with war. He earned the gratitude of the Duke of Wellington for coming to his assistance against the French in 1814.

At the end of the Napoleonic Wars, Penrose led the Mediterranean Fleet on two occasions, it being one of the most important commands in the navy at the time.

However, it was another man with Cornish connections – a man more famous than Penrose – who was in charge when the Bombardment of Algiers successfully secured the release of more than 1,000 Christian slaves in 1816. Admiral Lord Exmouth was created first Viscount Exmouth for his efforts. Exmouth – real name Edward Pellew – was not born in Cornwall, but the family was of Cornish descent and Edward attended Truro Grammar School. Younger brother Israel also enjoyed a distinguished career at sea, though did not gain the fame of his sibling.

'BLIGH' INTO THE FACE OF DANGER
The people of Cornwall could be forgiven for not trying too hard to claim Vice-Admiral William Bligh as one of their own.

Thanks to filmmakers, this Cornishman or Devonian (there has been much debate as to what side of the border he was born on) is not exactly a hero of maritime Britain. In fact, he is often seen as the villain – a cruel tyrant who got what he deserved when Fletcher Christian led the mutiny on the *Bounty* in 1789.

It is perhaps unfortunate that the image of Bligh – in the minds of most people – is solely based on the portrayals by the likes of Charles Laughton, Trevor Howard and Anthony Hopkins in the movies. No doubt Bligh was a strong leader, a strict disciplinarian, but then most captains had to be. And there are some historians who have actually suggested that Bligh was, in fact, not as tough and brutish as others in his position. Certainly, his log reveals that he was sparing when it came to handing out punishments. In fact, Bligh cared much about the welfare of his crew. He made sure that his men had a balanced diet and took exercise on a regular basis. He kept his ship in pristine condition, aware that poor sanitation led to illness. Indeed, there is no evidence that Bligh was any worse than other captains in making sure his high standards were met.

And yet it is the mutiny on the *Bounty* for which Bligh is remembered and little else. Sadly, the rest of the story of this talented seaman is not so often told.

Bligh was born for the sea, whether that was at the ancestral home of Tinten Manor in St Tudy, near Bodmin, or at Plymouth, where his father worked as a customs officer. Many go for the Devon option because Bligh was supposedly baptised in Plymouth, though, to be accurate, his baptism was only *registered* in that city – at the church where his parents were married – and may have taken place elsewhere. Bligh certainly believed himself to be Cornish, always insisting he was a native of St Tudy.

It is believed that Bligh was not even 10 when he got his first job at sea and steadily moved up the ranks. He served on HMS *Resolution* under the command of Captain James Cook, though his superior never came home, being killed in Hawaii.

Bligh did his time serving others and, in 1787, took command of the *Bounty*, the ship that made his name, for better or for worse. The aim of the ill-fated voyage was to gather breadfruit seeds from Tahiti and sail on to the West Indies, where the seeds were to be raised as a crop for the slaves. It is not known why Fletcher turned against Bligh. One theory is that the men became too idle and lost their discipline when bad weather resulted in the *Bounty* being stranded in Tahiti. When the ship finally set sail, the men may have had trouble readapting to the tough regime demanded at sea.

Bligh wrote in his logbook that he was asleep when Fletcher came into his cabin. He was put overboard in an open boat with some of his officers. He was given no charts and few supplies. Some 3,000 miles and six weeks later, the boat made it to Timor. All on board survived the ordeal, thanks to the skill and discipline of Bligh. Many have since claimed it as the greatest navigational feat of all time.

Bligh returned home in 1790. He was cleared of all blame for the mutiny and resumed his naval career. And, a couple of years later, he was back in Tahiti to complete the job. This time the breadfruit seeds were successfully delivered to the West Indies.

Bligh saw many battles during the remaining years of his career. Lord Nelson was among those who praised him for his bravery. He won many honours for his services to navigation and botany.

THE GREAT ESCAPE

If the epic voyage of William Bligh was the greatest navigational feat of all time, a similar odyssey made by Fowey-born Mary Bryant would run a close second. But what made her journey even more remarkable was the fact that she was no mariner – but a convict.

Not long after Bligh had made it safely to Timor, Mary did likewise. Convicted of a street robbery, she was banished to the penal colony established at Botany Bay in Australia. There she married and, along with her husband, her children and a number of fellow convicts, she hatched a daring escape plan. Their small boat reached Timor – a distance of more than 3,000 miles – some ten weeks after setting sail, much of the voyage taking place in unchartered waters. Despite enduring storms and hostile natives, it is believed all survived the journey. However, the convicts were rearrested in the East Indies and, ironically, brought home to England, at least part of the way, on a ship carrying some of the captured *Bounty* mutineers. Many of the convicts, including Mary Bryant's husband and children, died on the voyage home.

Mary was imprisoned at Newgate on her return. Her remarkable escape was considered just as great an achievement as that of Bligh and she became a national heroine. James Boswell, biographer of Samuel Johnson, championed her cause, claiming she had suffered enough, and she was eventually pardoned and freed in 1793.

WALLIS AND 'VOMIT'

The islands to which Samuel Wallis gave his name are probably more famous than the man himself. Many people would be able to locate the Wallis Islands on a map, but they would struggle to tell you much about the naval officer who discovered them.

However, Wallis served Britain with great distinction during times of war and, as an explorer, was responsible for adding a number of Pacific islands to our maps, including Tahiti.

Having distinguished himself during the Seven Years' War, Wallis, who was born at Lanteglos, near Camelford, took command of HMS *Dolphin* in 1766 for a two-year mission to look for land in the Pacific Ocean. It was during this voyage that he discovered Tahiti, naming it King George III Island in honour of the English monarch.

Wallis was very sick for most of his stay on the island. It was a couple of weeks before he was able to leave his cabin and then the island queen ordered her men to carry him to her house for treatment, which involved some young ladies giving him a massage. It is said the queen was sorry when it was time for the outsiders to go home. No doubt, Wallis was sorry too! Certainly, Wallis, despite being ill for most of his stay, wrote complimentary things about the island, his words helping to create the paradisiacal status that Tahiti still enjoys to this day.

Wallis was a protégé of Admiral Edward Boscawen and shared his view that the well-being of the crew was of vital importance, even if Wallis, it appears, was himself prone to sickness.

The mapping work of Wallis was put to good use by many later explorers who sailed in the same seas, including Captain James Cook.

TIME IS OF THE ESSENCE

Some men never needed to board a ship to make an impact at sea; Cornishman John Arnold was one of them.

Although not a sailor himself, Arnold played a major part in the maritime history of Britain. And, it is fair to say, his work helped make the high seas a safer place for those who did venture further afield.

Navigation was still a major challenge for explorers in the eighteenth century. Ships frequently ran aground when sailors became lost, with many losing their lives as a result. The big challenge of the day was to find a way to calculate longitude while at sea. The chronometer became the solution. John Harrison is credited with its invention, but Bodmin clockmaker John Arnold was the man who made it the success it was to become.

Arnold followed in the footsteps of his father in making watches. However, he was to earn a bigger reputation. His skill was in manufacturing small timepieces and, in 1764, he famously made the smallest ever repeating and striking watch set in a ring as a gift to George III. It was to make his name.

Fortunately for British mariners, Arnold was not content to stick at producing quirky watches; his real interest was timekeeping at sea. Harrison's marine chronometers were complicated and expensive, but Arnold came up with versions that were simpler and cheaper to produce. In pioneering the means for the mass production of marine chronometers, more and more sailors were able to benefit. Captain James Cook relied on an

Arnold timepiece on one of his voyages to the South Seas in the 1770s.

Another Cornishman, Robert Were Fox, a Falmouth Quaker and the father of diarist Caroline, came up with an aid for polar navigation in the nineteenth century. His interest in magnesium led him to produce a dipping needle compass that became of great use on voyages to colder climes.

MAKE A 'RUM' FOR IT

Navigational aids were not all that mariners felt unable to do without; a tot of rum became just as important to many. And one Cornishman certainly exploited that craving.

Penzance-born Lehman 'Lemon' Hart became the first official supplier of rum to the British Royal Navy. Sailors had long been given rum as part of their rations, the officers obtaining it from random suppliers, usually merchants who were trading at their latest port of call. However, the Admiralty decided to seek an official supplier. Hart had developed the family business started by his German grandfather, a rum merchant. However, he was now not only selling rum, but making it himself and his Penzance distillery came to the attention of the Admiralty. It declared that each seaman would be issued a measure of rum – provided by Hart's distillery – at sunset every day.

Hart became a success all over the world in the early nineteenth century, trading under the name Lemon Hart Rum. The company is still in business today.

PACKETS TAKING PACKETS

Not all ships leaving British shores in the eighteenth century went to war or in search of new lands. In Cornwall, thousands set off to do a different job ... to deliver the post.

In 1688, the Royal Mail chose Falmouth as its outgoing port for overseas mail. Thanks to explorers, the British Empire was expanding and the delivery of packets to distant lands was to become a booming business. Hence, the

Falmouth packets – the boats charged with delivering mail, cargo and even passengers – became world famous.

Indeed, Falmouth itself was transformed by its new role; for a time it was the only place in the country where overseas mail was shipped in and out. It prospered and almost became the information centre of the British Empire. It is said that, in the eighteenth century, only in London would you learn the news of the day any quicker.

The packets went all over the world, and the 'postmen' had more than angry dogs to worry about. The sea was a dangerous place. Britain was frequently at war during the eighteenth and early nineteenth centuries, and there was still the threat of pirates. The Falmouth packets were sometimes armed, but more often had to rely on their speed to escape danger. There were many reports of the mail ships being attacked by enemy vessels and privateers. The packets often carried bullion in great quantities, which proved to be the downfall of one in 1763. The *Hanover* was travelling from Lisbon to Falmouth with gold and other valuables. She was caught in a storm and, already heavily laden, veered up the north coast of Cornwall, eventually sinking off St Agnes. Hanover Cove, between St Agnes and Perranporth, now bears the name of the doomed ship.

One captain of a Falmouth packet became a national hero. William Rogers was on a voyage to the Caribbean in 1807 when his vessel was attacked by a French privateer. Despite being heavily outnumbered, Rogers refused to surrender and ended up taking control of the French ship. He towed his 'prize' home, to much acclaim.

The arrival of steam in the mid-nineteenth century eventually put an end to the Falmouth packets. Steamships were faster and less reliant on good weather.

FIRST WITH THE NEWS

It was not a Falmouth packet that brought home the news of victory following the most famous maritime battle in English history. That honour fell upon some Cornish fishermen.

Following the Battle of Trafalgar in 1805, HMS *Pickle* was sent home ahead of the rest of the British fleet to relay the good news. It was bound for Falmouth, but fishermen in Mount's Bay ensured that the people of Penzance would be the first in England to learn of the victory. They had met HMS *Pickle* at sea – before it had reached Falmouth – and wasted no time in racing to Penzance to let everyone there know of the triumph, but also of the sad news that Lord Nelson had lost his life. The mayor of Penzance announced the news from the balcony of the Union Hotel, while locals marched to nearby Madron Church, the church for Penzance at the time, to sound the bells in triumph. Even today, Madron celebrates the victory at Trafalgar with an annual parade and service. While this part of Cornwall celebrated, HMS *Pickle* finally reached Falmouth.

KEEPING THE ENEMY AT BAY

You might have expected the people of Cornwall to flee when another great enemy of England arrived in Cawsand Bay in 1815. However, the authorities had to keep them *away* from him!

On board the *Bellerophon* was Napoleon Bonaparte. However, his days as the 'terror of Europe' were over and he was now effectively a prisoner aboard the ship. He was being held temporarily in the English Channel until a decision could be made on his future, Napoleon having recently been defeated at Waterloo.

Boatloads of curious sightseers, from all over England, attempted to get a better look at the defeated emperor. It is said that there were so many vessels full of tourists lined up for a glimpse of the prisoner that it was possible to walk from Plymouth Hoe to Cawsand on their decks without getting your feet wet. Napoleon is said to have obliged the onlookers by dressing in his best uniform and waving to the cheering crowds. Armed picket boats were required to keep in order those who were more than just curious.

Napoleon boards the *Bellerophon*.

It was eventually decided that St Helena would become the new home of Napoleon, and Cornwall became the last county in England he ever saw.

8

RELIGION AND CULTURE

THE RISE OF METHODISM AND DEMISE OF A LANGUAGE

SINGING FROM A DIFFERENT HYMN SHEET

A religious census of the mid-nineteenth century declared that more than half of the population of Cornwall were Methodists.

That survey was conducted some 100 years after John Wesley – the founder of Methodism – first came to the county. In fact, the survey revealed that 60 per cent of Cornish residents claimed to be Methodists, with just 27 per cent professing to be Anglicans.

Now even the Church of England had to concede that Methodism had won the battle to fill the pews, with Henry Phillpotts, Bishop of Exeter, as early as 1831, admitting: 'Wesleyanism is the established religion of Cornwall.'

Indeed, the impact Methodism had on Cornwall cannot be overstated. It brought about a change in the way of life. The message of hope it provided appealed to the working classes, from fishermen to miners. And it gave people a new sense of morality, men now more willing to inhabit chapels than taverns. It is safe to say that thanks to John Wesley, Cornwall became a more civil place than the one he first set foot in.

'METHOD' IN THE MADNESS

It could be argued that Methodism in Cornwall was a revolution that prevented a revolution. Indeed, many historians have come to share the belief that if the Methodists had not come to the county when they did, the long-suffering Cornish might have taken things into their own hands.

John Wesley.

Methodism brought hope at a time of much despair and unrest. Life in Cornwall during the mid-eighteenth century was bleak for the average man. Landowners got wealthier exploiting the mineral-rich countryside, but the tin workers only got poorer. Their meagre pay and terrible working conditions gave them cause to complain. And some have suggested that the ordinary worker was on the very brink when brothers John and Charles Wesley first set foot in the county.

Methodism may or may not have prevented a revolution, but you cannot doubt that it was itself one. However, it was a revolution like no other witnessed in Cornwall.

There is little doubt that the duchy was in need of religious reawakening when Charles Wesley (he came to the county a month or so before his brother) first arrived in the summer of 1743.

Not only were people living in hardship, but they were also suffering from spiritual poverty as well. With many miners turning to drink in a bid to forget their woes, the inns were doing better business than the churches. The Church of England offered little to the average man and was uninviting. Anglicanism was deemed to be the preserve of the rich; Methodism became the religion of the people. While bishops rarely ventured from their jewel-laden churches, the Methodists made it their mission to go to the people, even if those people lived in isolated communities at the very end of the country.

John Wesley – the founder of Methodism and the greatest preacher of his age – is said to have journeyed more than a quarter of a million miles on horseback during his ministry. He continued preaching well into his eighties. He came to Cornwall some thirty times in total.

The Wesley brothers would preach wherever they were wanted – and sometimes where they were not. When there was no room to accommodate all those who wanted to hear their message of hope, they would – famously – preach in the open air. Their pulling power cannot be overstated; thousands would flock to hear John, in particular. One of his favourite preaching locations was Gwennap Pit, near Redruth, where more than 20,000 were sometimes in attendance.

The people of Cornwall took to Methodism and its message of instant salvation. It offered them security and comfort. But not all embraced it, especially at first. In fact, many were opposed to it in the strongest way. Charles – on that first visit to the county back in 1743 – had headed for St Ives where Methodism had arrived earlier that year. A Methodist sea captain named Joseph Turner had helped set up a religious society in the town and Charles was checking it out. Among those who stood in opposition was the local rector, who labelled followers of Methodism as 'enemies of the Church'.

Both Wesley brothers were frequently hounded out of communities by their opponents, even physically attacked by mobs, John being hit over the head during his visit to St Ives. John said himself that the war against the Methodists was fought more vigorously than the one against the Spaniards! However, the message was getting through and crowds continued to flock to hear it.

Nothing would deter the Wesley brothers. Charles wrote, in reference to a passage in the *Book of Revelation*: 'God hath now set before us an open door, and who shall be able to shut it?'

People continued to try, of course, but they were losing the battle. Exploited workers found a new sense of worth. Methodism preached salvation for all – rich and poor. All were equal before God and all had access to him. Many people gave up drinking and some even credit the fall in smuggling – a way of life in Cornwall – to the rise of Methodism.

Cornwall took to Methodism like no other county in England. Ordinary people became preachers and the message continued to spread, though 'ordinary' is not the word you would use to describe Billy Bray – the most famous Cornish Methodist of the nineteenth century.

THE KING'S SON

Billy Bray had more opportunity than most to become a drunkard – he lived above a beer shop. However, he put that life behind him to become the most noted – and probably the most eccentric – product of Methodism in Cornwall.

Bray was typical of converts to the new religion, being one of many miners who gave up alcohol for a new life as an evangelist. Methodism made preachers out of ordinary people, and many took to the streets and hills following their own conversion. Bray did likewise. 'Typical' convert he may have been, but 'typical' evangelist he certainly was not. He could not have been more different than most preachers of his time – literally singing and dancing his way to salvation.

Bray would use wit and humour to attract crowds – and they kept coming. People could not get enough of him and flocked to hear what he had to say – and to watch him dance.

He could not stop singing and dancing. He was a joker and, though only a little man, would praise God at the top of his voice. He shouted, he sang, he danced and he joked his way through his sermons. He 'won' souls through wit and laughter, rather than by scaring people into submission. He became known throughout Cornwall and beyond, as his memorial in the churchyard at Baldhu, near Truro, reveals: 'His memorable sayings and doings has made his name familiar as a household word in our own and other lands.'

Bray would probably be viewed as a fool today, but his strange behaviour was just him expressing his joy at being saved.

Even during his own time, people would often call him a madman. In reply, he would justify his unconventional behaviour by saying that he was not a madman, but a 'glad man'. He was just 'glad' to be a child of God. Following his conversion, Bray called himself the 'King's Son', now believing it his responsibility to do the work of his 'father'.

He certainly did that. Behind the jokes and merriment was an honest sincerity. He lived by faith and never worried when the cupboard was bare. He earnestly believed that God would provide for his needs. On one occasion, he brought home two homeless siblings and stated: 'I thought I'd bring them in and rear them up with ours. The Lord can as well feed them here as he can in the workhouse.'

Bray also built chapels – literally. He would not only fund the project – often relying on God to provide the money – but also roll up his sleeves and do the work himself.

It was all a far cry from his youth. Born in 1794 at Twelveheads, Truro, he was brought up by his devout and God-fearing grandfather. However, the young Bray went off the rails big time when he moved to Devon to work in the mines. He was known for his filthy language and drinking prowess. While living above a beer shop, he would drink until he was sick. 'I used to dread to go to sleep for fear of waking up in hell,' he later wrote. He returned home to Cornwall a drunkard and not even marriage helped sober him up. Finally, on one day in 1823, he conceded that enough was enough. His conversion to Methodism was no whim. He vowed on that day not to touch another drop of alcohol and was true to his word.

Following his dramatic conversion, it was no longer the drink that made Bray merry. Of course, those who witnessed him express his joy by singing, dancing and joking could have been forgiven for thinking he was *still* on the bottle.

KICK WITH THE OTHER 'FOOTE'

Methodism not only had its opponents, but also its scoffers, and one Cornishman in particular made a lot of money out of poking fun at the Methodists.

Truro-born Samuel Foote, actor and dramatist, mocked the Methodist movement in his famous play *The Minor*. The production initially flopped in Ireland, but when Foote revised it and introduced it to English audiences, it played to packed theatres.

Often labelled the first stand-up comedian – Foote had a gift of mimicry – he became both loved and feared, the Methodists not unique in being ruthlessly mocked.

To be fair to Foote, he could have a laugh at his own expense as well. Following a riding accident he had to have a leg amputated. Turning to his pen, he made light of his predicament by writing *The Devil upon Two Sticks* and *The Lame Lover*.

INDEPENDENCE DAY

It is perhaps no surprise that Cornwall should embrace an 'independent' religion; the county has become synonymous with the word 'independence'.

But while its people were breaking from the Church of England to take up Methodism, the eighteenth century also signalled the end of the very thing that gave the county its independence – its language. Indeed, nothing more than an independent language, one only spoken on its soil and nowhere else, will testify that a place is unique and different from the rest.

The rise of Methodism and start of the Industrial Revolution in the eighteenth century heralded a new dawn in the history of Cornwall, but at the same time, the Cornish language all but disappeared with the setting sun.

GOODBYE, DOLLY!

There are some advantages in being the last person alive to speak Cornish; and Dolly Pentreath, who supposedly held that honour in the eighteenth century, knew how to exploit them, seemingly having a lot of fun doing so.

Most now agree that there were others who could still speak Cornish following her death in 1777, but Dolly was the one who earned the title. And there are even some who dare to suggest that she did not even know much Cornish, but exploited the fact that if no one else knew any, she could say what she liked and no one would be any the wiser! Others suggest that she certainly knew how to swear in Cornish and, when asked by curious sightseers to say something in her native tongue – unbeknown to them – she would reply with a torrent of abuse. Of course, so long as she spoke with a smile, the tourists would go home happy!

The lasting fame of Dolly Pentreath, the daughter of a Mousehole fisherman, has everything to do with Daines Barrington, an antiquary who wrote an account of his meeting with her. Barrington came to visit Dolly to try to find out as much as possible about the dying Cornish language. He noticed that other people in the area understood her, but could not speak the language themselves. Barrington hoped that scholars would capture it while it was still a living tongue.

Dolly Pentreath.

Barrington was not successful, but Dolly certainly benefited from his writing. She became a subject of curiosity and more visitors descended upon the Mousehole area to meet her in person. Dolly became a tourist attraction and it appears she was happy to play along. She would charge people money to hear her speak Cornish. Whether it was true Cornish that came from her lips or whether those words were filth that few would want to hear in any language, Dolly certainly became a minor celebrity, making a bit of money in the process.

A memorial in her honour was erected at Paul in the nineteenth century; Prince Louis Lucien Bonaparte, a keen student of languages and the nephew of Napoleon, was invited to perform the unveiling.

Antiquarians had fun trying to find the 'last' speaker of Cornish. Even if others did continue speaking it after Dolly Pentreath, its end was near and, by the end of the eighteenth century, it had all but disappeared.

9

INNOVATION AND ADVENTURE

INVENTORS, SCIENTISTS AND EXPLORERS

FULL STEAM AHEAD

Many people view Cornwall as being the backwater of England. A twelfth-century versifier at the court of Henry II put forward that idea in less than poetic terms when he declared that the county was 'the fag end of the world'.

However, that certainly could not be said of Cornwall at the beginning of the nineteenth century, the duchy being at the heart of Britain's Industrial Revolution.

Initially, it was steam that powered that revolution. And in the midst of all that steam you would often find a Cornishman. Indeed, Cornwall has produced more than its fair share of inventors and scientists for a county of its size. By the beginning of the twentieth century, more than 300 Cornishmen or women were thought worthy to be included in the famous *Dictionary of National Biography*, the average number of entries for each county being fewer than 200.

HELD IN HIGH 'ESTEAM'

No other Cornish inventor – and there have been many – is held in the same esteem as Richard Trevithick. Every year, the people of Camborne – his home town – devote a day to celebrate his life and many achievements. His high-pressure steam engines powered industry, and there can be very few inside Cornwall who would not agree that he is its greatest son.

Indeed, many believe this giant (he was also physically an enormous man) of the Industrial Revolution was the true father of the railways. Of course, today, that title is usually bestowed upon the more famous George Stephenson, but it

Richard Trevithick.

was Trevithick who really got things moving. And some say he was even responsible for the first motor car.

Trevithick, who was born in 1771, was a big man, blessed with amazing strength, which earned him a fine reputation as an athlete and wrestler. However, he had brains as well as brawn. Trevithick came up with many inventions, but it is steam with which he will forever be associated. At the beginning of the nineteenth century, Trevithick came up with the first steam engine that could move on roads. He first publicly tested his Puffin' Devil – as it was nicknamed – at the end of 1801. It climbed a hill in his native Camborne, effectively becoming the world's first motor vehicle.

It was followed by a vehicle that could run on rails. However, Trevithick abandoned railway locomotives, leaving Stephenson to develop the Cornishman's ground-breaking achievements in steam locomotion and to take most of the glory.

James Watt was another to overshadow Trevithick. The two engineers got all 'steamed up' over high and low pressure. Watt was an advocate of low-pressure steam engines. However, much to the disdain of Watt, Trevithick was of the belief that 'strong' steam could be harnessed safely and set about doing so. Trevithick's high-pressure engines for pumping benefitted mines throughout Cornwall.

The inventions of Trevithick should have brought him as much fame as Stephenson and Watt, but perhaps he himself was partly to blame for that not being so. Trevithick was a brilliant, but disorganised man who had little or no business sense. He left England for South America in 1816, becoming a mining consultant, his high-pressure steam engines first being put to good use in the silver mines of Peru.

However, his dreams of becoming a wealthy man did not materialise and after many adventures abroad, Trevithick returned to England in 1827 just as broke as when he left. While the likes of Stephenson had cashed in, Trevithick never got back on his feet financially and died in poverty. He was buried in an unmarked grave.

Trevithick is not forgotten, at least not in Cornwall. His statue stands proudly in Camborne, while Trevithick Day is celebrated every year in the town. However, compared to the likes of Stephenson and Watt, Richard Trevithick has not gained – at least outside Cornwall – the recognition he deserves.

GREAT SCOT

It is perhaps no surprise that the residents of Camborne should honour Richard Trevithick once a year; he is one of Cornwall's greatest sons, after all.

However, neighbouring Redruth does likewise for another giant of British engineering, and that man – William Murdoch – is entitled to feel even more honoured than Trevithick. You see, Murdoch was not even Cornish, and that very fact says quite a lot. How many other non-Cornishmen can boast a day of celebration in their honour within the county every year?

So what did Scotsman William Murdoch do to win a place in the hearts of the people of Redruth? A plaque outside the former Redruth home of Murdoch – he lived there 1782–98 – reveals that two very significant events occurred in that humble building. It was here that Murdoch made the first locomotive and it was here that he invented gas lighting. It is difficult to say which achievement was the most important; both had a huge impact.

Murdoch came to Cornwall as an employee of Boulton and Watt, a firm that designed and manufactured stationary steam engines. It is said that Murdoch, as a young man, walked some 300 miles from Scotland to Birmingham to ask James Watt – his fellow Scot and by then famous steam engineer – for a job.

Murdoch was sent to Redruth to install and maintain Boulton and Watt engines that were used for pumping water out of Cornish tin mines. He set up an office and foundry in his Redruth house, becoming responsible for a number of innovations in the development of the steam engine.

Murdoch produced Britain's first working model of a steam carriage or road locomotive. It was successfully tested in his living room in 1784. At just 1ft in height, it was the first man-made machine to move around completely under its own power. Trevithick – who for a spell actually lived in the house next door to the dwelling once occupied by Murdoch – went on to develop the ideas of his one-time neighbour. As for Murdoch, he is, in fact, remembered more for his experiments with gas, which also took place in his Redruth home. Indeed, that very building is reputed to be the first domestic residence to be lit by gas. Ironically, Murdoch failed to obtain a patent and actually made no money from his gas lighting. Of course, others certainly benefited and gas went on to power the Industrial Revolution.

William Murdoch may not have had any Cornish blood in him, but you cannot blame the people of Cornwall for adopting him as one of their own.

BEAM WITH PRIDE
The task of pumping water from mines became the pre-occupation of most inventors and engineers during the Industrial Revolution. Cornwall became world famous for its beam engines.

Thomas Newcomen was the first to remove water from Cornish mines in the first half of the eighteenth century using his atmospheric engine, but it was James Watt who created the first true steam engine. However, a patent on his invention meant that other engineers were restricted in their work, being unable to make modifications to improve existing Boulton and Watt engines or to invent new ones – for fear they might infringe that patent. It meant many talented Cornish engineers were left frustrated.

One Cornishman who did successfully make an impact during the Watt era was Jonathan Hornblower, who invented the compound steam engine in 1781. Hornblower, born at Chacewater, near Redruth, was actually employed by Watt to assist him in the installation of Boulton and

Watt engines throughout Cornwall. Indeed, Hornblower himself later lost a court case over an infringement of the Watt patent.

Finally, when Watt's patent expired, Cornish engineers were free to show off their talents, with the result that there was an eruption of new ideas at the beginning of the nineteenth century.

Camborne-born Arthur Woolf, in particular, developed the innovations of Hornblower and gained a reputation for building the finest engines, though they were soon superseded by those of Richard Trevithick.

Cornwall was not short of innovative engineers and the county became renowned for its beam engines. The Hayle-based firm Harvey & Co. became famous all over the world for its high-quality products. Not only were Cornish engines the best, they were also the biggest. In the mid-nineteenth century, Harvey & Co. supplied the largest beam engine in the world to the Dutch government for the purpose of draining a lake. The Camborne-based Holman firm was another supplier of quality mining equipment at the time.

BEARER OF GOOD 'FUSE'

Mining has always been a dangerous occupation, and as the tin and copper mine industries boomed in Cornwall, many paid the ultimate price in attempting to extract these vital commodities.

As production in the first half of the nineteenth century increased, so did the number of accidents. There was little regard for the lives of miners; many died or were mutilated in explosions. The main problem was that 'controlled' blasts were not very well controlled!

That was at least until a factory in Tuckingmill, near Camborne, started to produce the invention of local resident William Bickford. One day in the early 1830s, Bickford watched rope being made by the twisting of

Miners had a hard and often short life.

separate strands. Having already tried to come up with a safe fuse for controlled explosions, he became convinced that he could adopt this same method, and set about designing a machine that was able to wind strands of jute around a central core of gunpowder. Unlike the unpredictable fuses already used in mines, Bickford's fuse – coated with varnish to make it waterproof – burnt at a steady rate. It meant that the man lighting it knew – by its length – how long he had to get clear of the explosion.

Bickford had invented the safety fuse and he himself travelled throughout the mines of Cornwall promoting his 'safety rods' – as he called them. Many miners still 'preferred' the old fuses – often made from straw or goose quills – because they were cheaper, but it is said that the Tuckingmill factory produced some 45 miles of Bickford's fuse in its first year of production. Sadly, Bickford died just before the factory opened, but it prospered without him and many miners went on to benefit from his legacy.

YOU CAN'T KEEP A GOOD MAN DOWN

Another invention that made mining safer also saw the light of day towards the end of the first half of the nineteenth century. In fact, the man engine – a device that carried miners up and down the shaft of a mine – *literally* saw the light of day, but only when it was time to bring the tired workers back to the surface again.

Cornishman Michael Loam is often credited with being the inventor of the man engine, though, in truth, his design was based upon a similar machine already in operation in Germany. However, Loam certainly gained the credit for introducing it to Cornwall. The first miners to benefit were those working at Tresavean Mine, near Redruth, Loam's man engine being installed there in 1842.

The man engine saved lives and time. Before its introduction, miners had to get to their place of work below the surface by foot and this might involve climbing down a ladder or taking a sloping tunnel. Sometimes it could take them about an hour. Tresavean Mine was one of the deepest in Cornwall at the time, reaching a depth of more than 450m. The man engine took approximately twenty-five minutes to reach the bottom. As most miners were only paid from the moment they physically started work and not while in transit, they would have appreciated the new device. And, of course, more importantly, the risk of death was significantly reduced by it. Climbing up and down a mine ladder would not have been for the fainthearted. Victorian writer Wilkie Collins famously had a go when he visited Botallack Mine, near St Just. He wrote:

> The process of getting down the ladders was not very pleasant. They were all quite perpendicular, the rounds were placed at irregular distances, where many of them were much worn away, and were slippery with water and copper-ooze. Add to this, the narrowness of the shaft, the dripping wet rock shutting you in … the fathomless darkness beneath … the consciousness that if the rounds

of the ladder broke, you might fall down a thousand feet
or so of narrow tunnel in a moment – imagine all this,
and you may easily realise what are the first impressions
produced by a descent into a Cornish mine.

Indeed, many a tired miner did lose his footing and fall to
his death. To emphasise how safe Loam's new man engine
was, schoolchildren were taken down.

It is safe to say that Loam's device helped save the lives of
many. However, accidents in mining are inevitable. In 1919,
the man engine collapsed at Levant Mine with the result
that thirty-one miners lost their lives. It was the greatest
loss of life in a Cornish mine since thirty-nine were killed
after heavy rain flooded East Wheal Rose Mine in 1846.

HE CLEANED UP

Not all men of enterprise got their hands dirty during the
Industrial Revolution, but one Cornishman came up with
something to help those that did. In the grimy and steamy
world of mining, there was certainly room for a bar of soap.

Andrew Pears (the name will have already given the
game away to some) became famous for producing a soap
that was pure and gentle to the skin, a complete contrast
to others available at the time. Later, with the help of very
successful advertising campaigns, Pears became a household name.

Most soaps available at the beginning of the nineteenth
century were harsh and rough. The soap of Andrew Pears
– based on glycerine and natural oils – was unique, being
transparent and scented with flowers. Despite being expensive, the novelty of the product made it very popular. People
were not put off by the price and could not get enough of it.

Mevagissey-born Pears was among the first to recognise
the importance of branding. Every bar of soap was lovingly
wrapped and signed by the man himself 'with my own quill'
– not stamped or printed.

'TITANIC' DISCOVERY

Many come to Cornwall to play in the sand, and duchy resident William Gregor also liked nothing better than to 'amuse' himself with it. It was typical of this humble clergyman that he should refer to his studies in chemistry as his 'amusement'. However, his experiments were a little more important than that.

In 1791, Gregor, who was rector of Creed, near Probus, was sent some black sand from the Manaccan valley on the Lizard peninsula. He concluded that the sand contained an unidentified white metallic oxide that did not match the properties of any known element. Gregor named it manaccanite after the place where it was found. He reported his findings to the geological experts, but no one did much about it. And Gregor, being an unassuming sort of person, never pushed it further. However, a German chemist then made a similar discovery. Believing himself to be the first, he named the metal titanium, due to the titanic grip that locks it into its compounds. When he realised that someone had actually beaten him to the discovery, he graciously gave Gregor the credit, though the name titanium stuck.

Of course, if Gregor had been a little more forceful when he made his remarkable discovery, the ninth most abundant element might have been named after a place in Cornwall.

MINING IN A NEW LIGHT

Some people rather harshly suggest that the greatest discovery of scientist Sir Humphry Davy was ... Michael Faraday.

Faraday, who was employed as an assistant to Penzance-born Davy, did perhaps go on to even greater things, but that is not to say that Davy did not himself achieve greatness. Indeed, many are of the opinion that Cornwall not only had the greatest engineer of the day in Richard Trevithick, but also the greatest scientist in Davy.

The fact that Davy is remembered for inventing the safety lamp for miners and little else is probably due to the fact that the average man on the street is unable to comprehend the importance of his contribution to science, in particular chemistry.

Davy discovered a number of previously unknown elements at the beginning of the nineteenth century, including potassium, sodium and calcium. Despite now being familiar to all, most people would not have any idea how being aware of their existence changed the course of chemistry. But, it is safe to say, the experiments and discoveries of Davy took it to a new level.

Of course, if Davy is solely to be remembered for his safety lamp then it is still not a bad legacy as it is impossible to estimate how many lives his invention has saved.

Davy had already made his name when he was approached to help the mining community in 1815. Explosions in mines were common and many lost their lives. Needing light to do their work, miners had no option other than to place a candle in their hats. However, the naked flame would often ignite the combustible gases found deep down in the mines. Davy designed a lamp that allowed only a small amount of air to reach the oil burner that was situated in a closed case.

Davy was a man of many talents. He was also a fine wordsmith. Some have suggested that if he had not become the greatest scientist of his time, he would have become the greatest poet. And that is some compliment when you learn that Coleridge and Wordsworth were among his literary friends. Davy even proofread their work.

Davy worked hard, but enjoyed the privileges his success afforded him; he was a man of the ladies. It is said many of the opposite sex came to his lectures and got all they wanted from the experience, despite not having a clue what he was talking about!

Despite his success, Davy was not always popular. Wordsworth was among those of the opinion that he should have concentrated more on his work than making an impression in society and flirting with the ladies. However, when you consider his achievements, perhaps this pioneering scientist can be forgiven.

Goldsworthy Gurney.

NO LONGER IN THE LIMELIGHT

Sir Goldsworthy Gurney was deserving of his place 'in the limelight'. After all, he was responsible for that very phrase. However, this remarkable inventor and scientist remains largely unheard of outside Cornwall these days and, some might argue, even within it. Gurney has retreated into the shadows of Cornish contemporaries Richard Trevithick and Humphry Davy, and that is perhaps ironic, because if anyone is deserving of remaining in the spotlight, then Goldsworthy Gurney is probably that man.

Gurney invented many things, but it was his experiments with light that particularly illuminated London – in more ways than one. It was Gurney who discovered the limelight effect: that an intense light could be produced when a piece of lime is heated in a flame of burning oxygen and hydrogen. Theatres were among the buildings to benefit from it, resulting in the phrase 'in the limelight', which is still used today to refer to those on stage or in the public eye.

Gurney also came up with the idea that an entire building could be lit from just one single point of light, using mirrors and prisms to reflect it.

The Bude Light – named after the north Cornwall town where Gurney spent his time when not in London – became a big hit. It was used to illuminate various London landmarks, including Pall Mall and Trafalgar Square, as well as the House of Commons, replacing the 280 or so candles that had previously done the same job.

Not surprisingly, Gurney illuminated his own Cornish home with his Bude Light. That house – Bude Castle – still stands today, though few believed it was even possible to build in the first place. Gurney, much to the amazement of everyone, chose Summerleaze Beach on which to build his home by the sea. It was generally considered impossible to build on sand. Gurney proved that was not the case. His home was built on a 'raft' of concrete and is thought to have been the first house constructed in this manner.

Gurney had been more interested in steam than light when he first left Cornwall to move to London, and it was his achievements in this area of science that made his name. In 1825, he registered a patent for 'an apparatus for propelling carriages on common roads or railways – without the aid of horses, with sufficient speed for the carriage of passengers and goods'.

Gurney went on to develop his steam carriage in the following years. Sadly, the increasing number of road tolls put an end to his once thriving enterprise and Gurney 'retired' to Bude to work on other things. However, his contribution to steam locomotion cannot be overstated. Gurney is also credited as having invented the steam jet and it was put to good use in many ways, such as in the ventilation of coal mines and cleansing of sewers.

However, it was not just in steam and light where Gurney made his mark. He was a versatile scientist and also influenced telegraphy.

The church at Poughill, the village near Bude where Gurney spent later years, contains a memorial that states 'his [Gurney's] inventions and discoveries in steam and electricity made communication by land and by sea so rapid that it became necessary for all England to keep uniform clock-time'.

Certainly, Goldsworthy Gurney – he was knighted by Queen Victoria for his contribution to science – was deserving of his time in the limelight and perhaps should still be there.

I KNOW A MAN THAT CAN

Davies Gilbert made a huge contribution to science; however, he is not remembered for being a scientist – even though he was himself an accomplished one – but for helping his fellow scientists achieve *their* goals.

It was fine coming up with scientific discoveries, but many scientists had no idea, or the means, to develop their science for the benefit of others. Gilbert became almost an administrator for scientists: they came up with the ideas and he turned them into reality. He put his vast knowledge of all things scientific at the service of others, not only offering advice, but giving his time and money as well, becoming a patron to many Cornish engineers.

Gilbert worked with Jonathan Hornblower and Richard Trevithick developing high-pressure steam engines, while many claim that Humphry Davy would not have become the man he did without the encouragement of Gilbert.

Gilbert was a member of various societies and also an MP. He was the unofficial representative of science in the House of Commons. Many scientists and engineers came to him for advice. A grateful Thomas Telford changed his design of the Menai Bridge after Gilbert – a top mathematician – pointed out a number of flaws.

Davies Gilbert may not be a name many have heard of today, but this much-admired Cornishman – he was born at St Erth, near Hayle, in 1767 – was the friend of all. He chaired committees for all sorts of projects, from lighting streets to strengthening harbours. If there was a practical problem, Gilbert believed science had the solution. As the ultimate networker, he may not have been able to personally come up with the answer himself, but, more often than not, he had a friend who could!

IT ALL ADDS UP TO A NEW PLANET

Mathematics can be put to great use in everyday life. If your children do not share that view as they struggle with their homework, you might like to point them in the direction of Cornishman John Couch Adams.

Adams shares the distinction of being the first man to discover the existence of a planet using only mathematics.

Astronomers in the 1840s could not work out why there were irregularities in the orbit of the planet Uranus. Adams did his sums and concluded that the cause of the erratic orbit could be found in a particular point in the sky. He believed astronomers only had to focus their telescopes on that point, and they would find another planet. They eventually did – and Neptune was discovered.

Adams was not alone in predicting the existence and position of Neptune using mathematics. French astronomer Urbain Le Verrier had come to the same conclusion at almost the same time. However, both Britain and France claimed that their man had done so first.

Adams was not bothered by the commotion that followed. Being a shy and modest man, fame meant nothing to him. He was just glad that he had been proved right.

The discovery of Neptune caused a sensation, particularly because of the way Adams and Le Verrier had set about finding it.

Adams, who was born at Laneast, near Launceston, went on to become one of the leading scientists of the nineteenth century, earning a reputation as both a brilliant astronomer and mathematician. He held various distinguished positions in later life, but supposedly turned down a knighthood and the prestigious post of Astronomer Royal.

OUT OF AFRICA

Space exploration was still a long way off in the days of John Couch Adams. However, there was still plenty to discover on *this* planet in the nineteenth century. The great Elizabethan explorers had made the world a 'smaller' place, but large parts of it still remained unchartered.

Outside of Cornwall, Richard Lander is not widely remembered. And even in his home town of Truro where his statue stands and where there is a school bearing his name, many are unable to tell you exactly what he did.

Lander was the man who discovered the source of the River Niger. That fact alone does not really do him justice, however. Somehow it does not seem as 'sexy' as discovering Australia or being the first to reach the South Pole. But Africa – in the days of Lander – was unknown and unmapped. In charting the entire length of the River Niger – some 2,600 miles – from its source to sea, Lander helped open up West Africa to the rest of the world. Trade links were established and eventually these new legitimate markets replaced the slave trade, the new visitors to Africa convincing local chiefs that instead of selling their people as slaves, there was more gain in using them to collect products for trading, such as palm oil.

Lander, the son of a Truro innkeeper, was destined to become an explorer. Full of adventure from an early age, it is said that he was only 9 when he walked to London to seek employment with the explorers of the day. He had visited most of the known world by the time he had reached his twenties.

Lander made three exhibitions to Africa. The first expedition in 1825–28 – working for Scottish explorer Hugh Clapperton – was a disaster. Clapperton and most of the party died after catching a fever; Lander had to find his way back to the coast alone, a journey that took him many months. On the way back, Lander was captured by natives and accused of being a witch. He was only freed after surviving a trial that involved drinking poison. That thrilling adventure made him a hero among the ordinary people. On the back of his new-found popularity, Lander managed to persuade the government to fund a second expedition. This time he went with his younger brother. The aim was to set up trading links, and to root out slavery and human sacrifice, something that abhorred the brothers. On their return, having survived more adventures, including being kidnapped, the Landers published their journal and maps. Richard Lander became the first man to receive the Royal Geographical Society's Gold Medal.

Lander would not rest on his laurels. He went back to Africa for a third time, but was shot in the leg during an ambush. The wound never healed and he died, aged just 29.

ROOTING AROUND
Not all explorers set sail in a bid to establish trading links or to abolish slavery – some merely went to pick flowers!

To be fair to Cornish brothers William and Thomas Lobb, they did a bit more than that really. Plant-hunting was big business in the nineteenth century and the Lobbs made a very significant contribution.

Both brothers went all over the world to collect seeds of different living things. They brought back exotic plants that we now take for granted, such as the monkey puzzle tree and giant redwood, plus a range of rhododendrons and orchids.

William went west to the Americas on his travels and Thomas went the other way, to the Far East.

THE FIRST FARMER OF AUSTRALIA
Some people did not travel to foreign shores by choice. James Ruse was *forced* to make the long trip to Australia

towards the end of the eighteenth century, arriving in New South Wales on the first fleet of convict ships.

Ruse, who was born at Lawhitton, near Launceston, is often described as the very first settler in Australia, having persuaded the governor of his new home to give him a small piece of land to produce food for the colony. With food in very short supply, his request was granted and Ruse, who had been convicted of burglary, made a success of his 'farm' – showing the authorities that it was possible to be self-sufficient. He was granted a bigger piece of land, and this pioneering farmer turned from villain to hero, one of the top agricultural colleges in Australia now bearing his name.

EMPIRE OF THE BODMIN 'SON'

It is difficult for the people of Bodmin to forget adventurer Sir Walter Raleigh Gilbert as they are reminded of him by a 144ft memorial on a hill overlooking the town. And yet this one-time hero of the nation is little remembered elsewhere.

Of course, colonisers such as Gilbert are no longer celebrated as they were when the British Empire was looked upon with pride and not shame, as is often the case today.

Gilbert, who was born in Bodmin in 1785, spent most of his life as a military commander in India. He won the admiration of the people of England for his role in the wars against the Sikhs in the first half of the nineteenth century, becoming known as the man who conquered the Punjab. The government issued a medal bearing his portrait, making him the only general, except the Duke of Wellington, to have his face on a military medal.

Gilbert was a descendant of two Elizabethan explorers, his name offering more than a clue as to which two!

'PEARD' THE LION

Cornish soldier John Whitehead Peard not only fought on foreign soil – but for the cause of a foreigner to boot.

Peard was known as 'Garibaldi's Englishman'. He joined Garibaldi in 1859, organising a company of volunteers to aid the famous nationalist. And Garibaldi claimed that Italy would never have been won if it were not for his English legion and its gallant colonel.

Peard and Garibaldi possessed similar features and were often mistaken for the other, something they put to good use on at least one occasion in a bid to confuse the enemy.

BISHOP BELIEVED IN THEM

Some Cornish adventurers are held more dearly in foreign lands than at home. Bishop John Colenso certainly fits that bill. Now largely unknown in Cornwall, his name is still revered in South Africa.

St Austell-born Colenso was appointed the first bishop of the new colony of Natal in 1853. His good work among the Zulu people was overshadowed by his controversial beliefs, which outraged his superiors and the orthodox believers in his own country.

Colenso helped build hospitals, schools and churches. He not only learnt the language of the Zulus, but also gave it its spellings and grammar. He created a Zulu dictionary and translated the Bible, so that his Zulu converts could read it in their own language.

However, his own radical beliefs led to a charge of heresy. As an advocate of higher criticism, he held the view that not all the Bible was the literal truth or historically accurate.

Colenso remained in Natal until his death. He caused more controversy by denouncing the Anglo–Zulu War, which broke out in 1879.

10

INDUSTRY

TIN TO TELECOMMUNICATIONS

'COPPER' LOAD OF THIS

Bring up the subject of mining in Cornwall and most people will immediately think of tin, and most wrongly assume it was tin that made the county the world leader in hard-rock mining during the late eighteenth and nineteenth centuries. However, that honour must go to copper.

Tin may have been mined in Cornwall longer than copper, but it was really copper that became the mainstay of Cornish mining in the nineteenth century. More than double the amount of copper as opposed to tin was produced in the county during the most prosperous years. At its peak in the mid-nineteenth century, it is estimated that copper production rose to somewhere in the region of some 200,000 tonnes a year.

It is difficult to put an exact date on the beginning of the copper boom in Cornwall. It is not even clear when mining for copper started. However, by the late eighteenth century, the parish of Gwennap – considered the home of copper mining – was labelled as being in possession of 'the

Copper being mined at Dolcoath in Camborne.

richest square mile to be found anywhere on the Earth'. Of course, Gwennap was not alone in prospering from the rich reserves of copper ore found below Cornish soil. Significant discoveries of copper were found elsewhere in the county, and Cornwall – until at least 1840 when it was overtaken by Chile – had the distinction of being the world's largest producer, supplying two-thirds of the planet's output.

While tin was smelted in Cornwall, copper ore was mostly shipped to South Wales. The ships would return with the coal that was needed to power the steam engines used for the extraction of the ore. Mining for copper proved to be far more lucrative than the extraction of tin, but, by the mid 1860s, the good days were well and truly over. Discoveries of copper ore in other parts of the world brought prices down and many Cornish mines were forced to close.

In truth, the Cornish copper industry had been in decline before then and some mines as early as the 1830s had already turned their attention to deep tin, using new improved machinery that allowed them to delve even further below the ground. Those far-sighted mine owners were the lucky ones and helped to cushion the blow inflicted on the Cornish mining industry through the copper crash.

However, many were not so lucky and many miners were forced to move to foreign shores to survive.

HOME FROM HOME

An old Cornish saying declares that wherever you find a hole sunk in the ground – you will find a Cornishman at the bottom of it. Said in jest it may have been, but you can understand why people expressed that thought.

During the nineteenth century, scores of Cornish miners left home to try their luck on foreign shores. Indeed, you might have come across a Cornishman in many parts of the world: South America, Latin America, North America, South Africa and Australia, in particular. Wherever there were mines, there was a good chance that Cornishmen were working down them.

The Cornish miners were not the first to look for a better life away from the duchy. Farmers, merchants and even those seeking greater religious freedom had gone before them, but it was the departure of thousands of miners that took emigration from Cornwall to an unprecedented high. In fact, more people left Cornwall than any other county in England during this period. It is said that at least a fifth of Cornish men migrated abroad every year during the last four decades of the nineteenth century.

The reason for this mass migration is not difficult to understand. The 1860s was the decade in which the traditional mining industries of Cornwall started to decline. Mines were closing. A total of twenty closed in 1866 and it is said that more than 10,000 miners lost their jobs in the following year. The rest of the world was catching up with Cornwall and the county struggled against increasing competition from foreign companies.

It meant Cornish miners were forced to look elsewhere for a job. They had the skills and many saw emigration as their best option. Foreign mines used agents to recruit Cornish miners, and husbands would often leave their families behind. There are many different versions as to how the Cornish miners became known as 'Cousin Jacks' to their new employers. Some say that when a Cornish miner was asked whether he knew of someone who could do a particular job, he would more often than not reply that he would send home for 'Cousin Jack'. It is suggested that the nickname came about because the miners addressed each other using the old Cornish term of 'cousin' and it just happened that the most common Christian name at the time was 'Jack'. Their wives became known as 'Cousin Jennies'.

Of course, emigration was not as easy as it is today. Just getting to foreign shores was a challenge. Newlyn was the starting point of an incredible feat of seamanship in 1854, in which seven men set sail for the Australian goldfields in nothing more than a 36ft fishing boat called the *Mystery*. Travelling with just the basic navigational aids, it took them 115 days to reach Melbourne. It is believed that the *Mystery* was at the time the smallest sailing boat ever to have completed such a journey.

Cornish miners played a huge part in the development of hard-rock mining in various parts of the world. The industries of copper, silver, gold and even diamonds thrived thanks to the expertise of nineteenth-century Cornish emigrants. Their influence remains even to this day in some places. Statues and memorials honour their work, while in Moonta, Australia, there is even a biennial Cornish festival that attracts thousands of people. And, of course, you will now find the 'Cornish' pasty in the most unlikely places, thanks to the miners who – despite being hundreds of miles from home – could not do without their favourite bite.

EASY MEAT

The Cornish are proud of their pasties, and people cannot get enough of them. In fact, it is estimated that a staggering 120 million Cornish pasties are consumed every year.

Of course, they are only 'Cornish' pasties if they are made in Cornwall. The EU officially declared that fact in 2011 after much legal wrangling.

The pasty has been around for centuries, but it was the Cornish miners who adopted it and made it their own. There is little doubt that they were responsible for making the pasty what it is today: not only the 'national' dish of Cornwall, but a cheap and convenient snack that is enjoyed all over Britain.

It was not like that in the thirteenth century, thought to be the earliest that pasties can be found on record. In fact, in those days they were the preserve of the rich. Venison and even seafood, such as eels, proved popular fillings. Certainly, they were not meant for the man on the street or the man down a mine.

There is no conclusive proof that the Cornish miners were responsible for making the pasty one of the first convenience foods. However, it is easy to see why it may have taken off within the mining community. Working deep underground brought many problems, including the dilemma of what to do for lunch. It was not convenient to pop down the local, and most miners did not see daylight again until they had finished their shift. Traditionally, the pasty that became their lunch contained two courses: savoury and sweet. Unlike the pasties eaten by the upper class, it was unlikely those consumed by the miners contained any meat, that being too expensive an ingredient. Potato, swede and onion – all cheap vegetables – were the most likely fillings for the savoury half of the pasty, while the sweet half would more often than not contain a stuffing of fruit. The crescent shape of the pasty made it easy to carry and some argue that the crust was merely meant to be used as a handle and not eaten. Washing your hands before your meal would not be possible and, with traces of arsenic from the ground likely to be on your fingers, the idea of discarding that 'handle' made good sense. However, many scoff at that notion and photographs frequently picture miners eating their pasties wrapped in cloth or within paper bags.

It is said that the ingredients inside the Cornish pasty would stay warm for hours. The women would even mark the initials of their husband on the pastry, so that each individual miner did not have to eat it all at once and would know which was his when he came back to it later in the day.

Some Cornish mines – such was the popularity of the pasty – installed stoves in the mine shafts. A mine manager, quoted in an 1864 report on the condition of mines in Britain, pointed out: 'We have four mine establishments with an oven in each of them, large enough to contain two hundred pasties or hoggans.'

This is reputedly where the chant 'Oggy, Oggy, Oggy' originates from, 'Oggy' stemming from 'hoggan' – a type of Cornish pasty eaten by the miners. The miners would know when the hoggan was ready to eat when they heard the call 'Oggy, Oggy, Oggy' from above. In reply, they would shout 'Oi, Oi, Oi'.

SITTING ON A 'COPPER' MINE

Mining made many men rich. William Lemon was among the far-sighted mine owners of the early eighteenth century to install the latest Newcomen engine for pumping water. It resulted in greater efficiency and was effectively responsible for the beginning of copper mining in Cornwall on a huge scale. It also made Lemon a fortune, and the family became one of the most prominent in Cornwall, in Truro in particular.

The Williams family of Scorrier also prospered from mining. John Williams managed many mines and by the start of the nineteenth century was in control of almost the entire Gwennap copper-belt – the richest area for copper in Cornwall at the time.

Williams was a leading authority on mining and many important people visited to pick his brains. Like Lemon, he also apparently had the gift of foresight. Williams had a recurring dream of the assassination of Prime Minister Spencer Perceval, but was talked out of warning him.

Joseph Treffry was known as the 'king of mid-Cornwall' because of the number of mines he owned in that area. On his death in 1850, it is said he was the biggest employer in the county. His money financed the famous viaduct at Luxulyan.

The cash of various mining magnates was used to construct harbours and piers throughout Cornwall for the benefit of the industry. Charles Rashleigh built a harbour at St Austell that became Charlestown – the new port being named after him – to export copper and later china clay.

Many magnates did much for their communities. Banker Humphry Millett Grylls is honoured with a memorial at Helston for his efforts in securing funding to keep Wheal Vor Mine open during tough times. It is said that some 1,000 families were saved from starvation through his intervention.

It is fair to say that benevolent mine owner Francis Basset is better known for his memorial than for what he achieved. It stands at the summit of Carn Brea, a hill overlooking Redruth. His achievements included raising an 'army' of miners to defend Plymouth from the combined fleets of France and Spain, but he also became a prominent politician and did much to improve working conditions.

The influence Basset had on people is perhaps highlighted by the fact that all the mines were closed on the day of his funeral and some 20,000 people formed the procession in Tehidy Park, the family home for centuries. His monument was paid for by the public. The mining community was not exactly forced to contribute, but was reputedly warned that the first three miners who failed to subscribe to the memorial fund would never work in Cornwall again!

DIAMOND GEEZER

Hard-up miners must have been very envious of their bosses; however, Francis Oats had the answer – he became one of them.

Oats, who was born at Golant, near Fowey, started life as a humble miner, but became one of the world's most powerful men in mining.

Having worked his way up to become captain of Botallack Mine, Oats moved to South Africa and continued to climb the career ladder, reviving the fortunes of the struggling Victoria Mine company. He kept going up until he became chairman of De Beers, the diamond mining company founded by Cecil Rhodes, which had the near monopoly of the international market.

QUEEN OF ROCK

It was not tin or copper that made one part of Cornwall rich; the Lizard peninsula became famous for serpentine – and still is.

The stone became fashionable during Victorian times, but even today most of the souvenir shops are almost entirely devoted to selling one thing – serpentine ornaments.

The industry gained the royal seal of approval when Queen Victoria visited in 1846. She purchased a number of serpentine products. Good enough for Queen 'Vic', it was good enough for all, and business boomed.

To satisfy growing demand, a factory was set up at Carleon Cove, Poltesco. A quay was even constructed at the mouth of the stream to enable the finished ornaments to be shipped to London and the Continent.

While Queen Victoria helped the people of The Lizard fill their pockets, spare a thought for local resident Sir Richard Vyvyan. He built Tremayne Quay, on the Helford River, solely for the purpose of receiving the monarch on one occasion. He knew it would leave him out of pocket, and he did not exactly get a good return for his efforts – the queen failing to turn up. The reputed reason: it was raining.

Queen Victoria.

The Lizard peninsula later benefited from the extraction of gabbro from Dean Quarry, near St Keverne. At its peak, more than 200,000 tonnes a year was being produced, the rock mostly used for the production of roads in the twentieth century.

The De Lank Quarry in Bodmin gained a reputation for producing some of the finest granite in the world. Its stone has been used to build many famous London landmarks, including Trafalgar Square.

FASHIONABLY 'SLATE'
A quite different type of rock helped make another part of Cornwall prosperous. Delabole, near Camelford, is home to the oldest working slate quarry in England.

It has been in operation for some 800 years, producing an estimated 10 million-plus tonnes of slate. The huge quarry, with a circumference of some 1.5 miles, was thought to be once the largest man-made hole in Europe.

WHAT LIES BENEATH
You never know what you might find down a Cornish mine, and many people are unaware of the fact that some mines in the county were excavated for uranium in the late nineteenth century and beyond.

South Terras Mine, near St Austell, was not only mined for uranium, but also radium, which was used in the research work of Marie Curie.

Other 'treasures' found below Cornish soil, to name but a few, include zinc, lead, arsenic, cobalt, nickel, silver and even gold.

THE MAN WHO STRUCK 'WHITE GOLD'
Sometimes you look far and wide for something – only to discover what you want is actually on your doorstep; this can be said of William Cookworthy.

He was the man who discovered china clay in Cornwall during the mid-eighteenth century. His discovery led to a booming industry that put the county at the forefront of porcelain manufacture. And as the copper and tin industries started to decline, it became a godsend for many Cornish families. Indeed, it is said that by the beginning of the twentieth century, Cornwall was producing more than a million tonnes of china clay every year, which gave it a virtual monopoly on world supply.

Cookworthy – a chemist with a fascination for geology – could have only dreamed of such a thing. His vision of making porcelain in England was hampered by the fact that he did not have the necessary materials to hand. At first he had to look overseas for samples of china clay to use in his experiments. The Chinese had been creating porcelain using kaolin (china clay) for centuries, but it was thought that kaolin was only found in that part of the world. On hearing that a similar substance had been discovered in Virginia, Cookworthy – a Quaker by religion – sent an associate to America to get him some. Businessmen from Virginia continued to supply Cookworthy with samples in an attempt to persuade him to import it. However, that would be costly and Cookworthy set about finding comparable minerals a little closer to home.

He did not have to look far. Being based in Plymouth, Cornwall was on his doorstep and, unbeknown to him at the time, a far more superior substance to the one he had been obtaining from Virginia was there for the taking.

Cookworthy first struck 'white gold' – a nickname for china clay – at Tregonning Hill, between Helston and Penzance, in the mid 1740s. However, greater quantities of a better quality were later discovered in other areas of Cornwall, notably north of St Austell, which was really the home of the Cornish china clay industry.

That industry became a powerful economic force. The evidence of its success is there for all to see, the waste from some 120 million tonnes of china clay thought to have been extracted since Cookworthy made his discovery now forming a lunar landscape of giant white peaks.

The 'Cornish Alps' – as this area is nicknamed – is perhaps now more famous for being the home of the Eden Project, the popular tourist attraction constructed within one of the abandoned china clay pits.

THIS IS THE AGE OF THE TRAIN
Copper and tin ores can be heavy; the mules of Cornwall in the late eighteenth and early nineteenth centuries would have discovered that fact.

It was great that men were able to extract copper and tin (thousands and thousands of tonnes of it) from the bowels of the Earth, but not so great if you were a mule and asked to carry it. Getting the minerals from the ground was one thing, but it was another to then get them to the people who were willing to pay for them.

There were not even decent roads for the mules to traverse, just stony tracks, and as we all know, Cornwall is not the flattest county in England. As well as bringing relief to those overworked mules, the arrival of the railway undoubtedly played its part in making the county a world leader in hard-rock mining. As more and more mines opened, the more important the railway became.

Cornwall got its railways because of the mining industry. They were not built to get *people* from A to B, but goods. Passenger travel was not even on the Cornish radar. All that mattered was finding a way of transferring ores from the mines to the harbours and ports.

Underground tramways existed in Cornish tin mines before the beginning of the nineteenth century. However, it was the rise of copper mining that led to tramways and railways being built above ground, though these at first were still horse-drawn and only moved goods short distances.

The Portreath Tramway had the honour of being the first railway above ground in Cornwall, starting operation in 1809. It later became known as the Poldice Tramway when it was extended to take in the mine of that name.

It was the first of a number of independent railway lines built specifically to carry minerals to the coast. The Poldice Tramway never carried passengers, at least not officially, and no steam locomotives ever ran on it. Horses or mules still had to do the leg work, but pulling wagons along rails was not as tough as carrying loads up and down rocky paths.

The Redruth and Chasewater Railway was regarded by many to be the first true railway in Cornwall, as this line did start to carry steam locomotives in the mid 1850s. It opened in 1826, being built to connect the mines of Gwennap with the coast. It made Devoran one of the most important ports in Cornwall. Ironically, the branch to Chacewater (the modern spelling) was never built.

The first line to use steam locomotives from its inception was the Bodmin and Wadebridge Railway. Its first locomotive – which started operation in 1834 – was named *Camel* after the river the line ran along and not the animal. However, the manufacturers supposedly did not realise that fact and called the second locomotive *Elephant*! The Bodmin and Wadebridge Railway was also the first to be built for imports, rather than exports. Its purpose was to carry sand from the coast to be used as a fertiliser on fields.

However, it was the mining industry that really benefited from the new railways. Because most were built to serve that industry, Cornwall was the last county in England to be connected to the national railway system. However, once the county did finally link up with the rest of the country, tourism was able to prosper and ultimately take the place of the declining mining industry.

THE CORNISH RIVIERA
Cornwall at the beginning of the nineteenth century was a remote place; the quickest way to reach London was by ship.

However, it is no surprise that it took so long for Cornwall to get a rail connection with the rest of the country: its population was sparse and there was generally no need or desire for people to visit the duchy.

It was not until 1859 that it became possible to travel to and from the capital by train. Thanks to the Great Western Railway (GWR) and Isambard Kingdom Brunel, its famous engineer, trains could at last cross the River Tamar, with the building of a new bridge. And it was worth the wait; the impact extending the national railway westward had on Cornwall cannot be overstated. Towns that sat on the line developed and those not connected to it fell into decline. Business boomed as goods could be in the capital much quicker than before. The fishing industry was one that particularly benefited, the fish still fresh when it reached the London markets.

However, it was tourism that really took off, and it was the GWR that deserves most of the credit. Some, in fact, argue that without the railway, Cornwall would not have become what it is today – with thousands heading to the duchy year after year for their holidays.

The name 'Cornish Riviera' – still much used today – was the invention of the GWR. It conjures up images of sandy beaches and blue seas, secret coves and sunny skies. And that is what Cornwall is about for most visitors. The GWR publicity and marketing department succeeded in getting across that message, and summer Saturday trains brought families by the bucket (and spade) loads.

Of course, most visitors today come to Cornwall by car. However, a reminder of that golden age of rail travel is found in one of the most famous trains still in operation: the Cornish Riviera Express. It still takes passengers from London to Penzance.

And while the railway may not bring most visitors to the county these days, there is little doubt that it played a huge part in bringing them here in the first place.

USE THE RAIL FOR HANGING!
You could be forgiven for thinking that the first excursion trains in Cornwall would have headed for the seaside. After all, that is where most visitors to the county wish to end up.

However, the Bodmin and Wadebridge Railway – the first in the county to officially carry passengers – came up with a novel day trip: to view executions at Bodmin Jail.

Even before tourism entrepreneur Thomas Cook was promoting his special excursion trains, the enterprising Bodmin and Wadebridge Railway had come up with the idea of cashing in on a popular form of 'entertainment'.

The company started to offer a special service to the jail on execution days. With public hangings in Britain often attracting huge crowds in the nineteenth century, the 'execution excursions' gave those from outside Bodmin the chance to participate in the 'fun'. The railway line ran alongside the jail and the packed train would actually stop directly opposite in order to give passengers a grandstand view of the proceedings.

BRIDGE OF 'SIZE'

Most holidaymakers come to Cornwall by car these days. That fact is emphasised by the presence of two bridges over the River Tamar; a modern road bridge now running parallel to the famous railway bridge built by Isambard Kingdom Brunel in 1859.

Of course, the car was not an option in the mid-nineteenth century. And, of course, the first tourists who did head to the south-west for their holidays could go no further than Devon. It was not until Brunel's Royal Albert Bridge extended the railway into Cornwall that the duchy became a holiday destination. Indeed, it is safe to say that Brunel was the man really responsible for bringing the tourists to Cornwall. Within six weeks of the bridge opening, Thomas Cook was organising holiday railway trips into Cornwall.

Brunel was also among the first 'tourists' to benefit from the extended railway. Having missed the official opening ceremony for the bridge due to ill health, Brunel – knowing he was dying – did fulfil his wish to cross the Tamar by train a few weeks later, in a special open truck made for the engineer.

The Royal Albert Bridge, at more than 2,000ft long, took almost six years to build. It was an incredible feat of engineering, Brunel having to provide at least 100ft headroom for ships, the clearance demanded by the Admiralty. It was Brunel's final project and some say his best.

INCLINED TO TRAVEL

The arrival of the railway signalled the end of the canal age. Not that Cornwall had that many in the first place, most being concentrated in the east of the county, the mining districts in the west served by tramways.

The geography and terrain of Cornwall proved to be a hindrance to engineers. However, Cornishman John Edyvean came up with a solution in hilly country, when he developed an inclined plane system in the 1770s, which avoided the need for locks. Edyvean was among the first to put forward a scheme for a canal at Bude on the north coast. Sand from the beaches there was used as agriculture fertiliser and needed to be transferred inland. Sadly, Edyvean died long before the canal was eventually built, but a series of inclined planes was indeed used to raise the boats between the various water levels, making it one of the most unusual canals in the country.

LET'S GO DOWN THAT ROAD

It was to be a long time before the road replaced rails as the most popular way to travel into Cornwall.

However, even before Isambard Kingdom Brunel completed his famous railway bridge, the duchy roads were improving.

One man responsible for that was Scotsman John Loudon McAdam. He came to Cornwall at the end of the eighteenth century after being asked to improve the road surfaces in Falmouth and the surrounding area, which he did utilising Cornish greenstone, among other things. He only stayed in Cornwall for a short time and most of his pioneering work in making roads more durable took place elsewhere, but it has been claimed that the duchy was the first place to benefit from a 'macadam' road. Named after McAdam himself, the roads became famous all over and were the forerunners to tar-bound roads, known as 'tarmacadam' – and now simply referred to as tarmac.

A FISHY TALE

Cornwall is more about tourism than fishing these days. However, like mining, the fishing industry helped make the county what it is today. And, for many visitors, it is the pretty fishing villages that make Cornwall so special, reeling tourists in year after year.

Cornish fishing villages owe their very existence to one particular fish – the humble pilchard. Pilchards were responsible for the development of almost all of the county's coastal villages. Millions of barrels were exported from Cornwall to the Mediterranean and other areas during the eighteenth and nineteenth centuries. It was big business – very big.

St Ives was considered the centre of the seine net pilchard fishing industry. At its peak, there were reports of single nets catching millions of pilchards at a time.

The fishing villages themselves are not the only physical evidence of a once thriving industry. The Huer's Hut at Newquay is perched on the cliff overlooking the bay. It affords a fine view out to sea – and that was why it was built there. Huers were lookout men; they would stare at the surface of the water for any signs of an approaching shoal of pilchards. The huer would alert the fishermen, who would drop everything and race to their seine boats. Sometimes using semaphore signals, the huer, from his position high above, would direct those in the boats, so that the shoal could be surrounded and netted.

Most of the pilchards were exported, the majority going to Italy. Many were sold on the Cornish shore, while pilchard oil helped fuel lamps. Even the poor-quality pilchards were not wasted, often used by farmers as a fertiliser.

By the mid-nineteenth century, the pilchard industry was in decline and drift fishing had taken over. The pilchards no longer frequented the Cornish coast in such big numbers and, looking at the size of some of the catches recorded in Cornwall, you could be forgiven for thinking that there were no pilchards left.

Pilchard fishing was a phenomenon almost exclusive to Cornwall. While the county remains a big player in the UK fishing industry today – Newlyn is home to one of England's largest fishing fleets – things are, of course, very different.

Now tourists have replaced the pilchards … and come in almost as great a number!

FISH IN TROUBLED WATERS

Regional rivalry within the fishing industry is nothing new. Faced with regulations and dwindling stocks, you cannot blame fishermen for being protective of 'their' waters, and that was certainly the case in Cornwall at the end of the nineteenth century.

Many have blamed the infamous Newlyn Riots of 1896 on the coming of the railway. More and more fishermen from the east and north of England were trying their luck in Cornish seas. With a rail service now between Cornwall and the capital, there was no need for the 'foreign' fishermen to travel back at night to ensure their catch was in the London markets by the morning. Just like the Cornish, they could use the train to deliver their goods. Traditionally, the Cornish drifters fished by night, but now they had to share their waters with the 'foreigners' who were in no rush to get home after dark. The easy access to the London markets attracted boats from even further afield, sometimes much bigger drifters, which were able to take an even larger share of the catch.

Tensions increased. The 'foreign' trawlers were accused of fouling Cornish drift nets and soon things boiled over. Many suggest the breaking point among the Cornish was the fact that the 'foreigners' also fished on Sundays. Most Cornish fishermen – many being strict Methodists – would not think of doing such a thing.

And so, on a Monday morning in 1896, the long-suffering fishermen of Mount's Bay snapped, physically attacking their rivals as they came ashore at Newlyn. A mob of more than 1,000 fishermen and their supporters seized the 'foreign' boats and destroyed their catches of mackerel. The riots lasted three days, the military eventually being required to intervene.

THE VILLAGE THAT DIED

It was not only the pilchards that vanished in Cornwall, the residents of a fishing village disappeared as well in the nineteenth century.

However, what really happened to the folk of Port Quin – sometimes known as 'the village that died' – is something of a mystery.

According to local legend, the whole population of this village near Port Isaac on the north coast disappeared overnight, reputedly leaving possessions and even food on their tables. Theories put forward include the idea that the residents drowned trying to help a shipwreck, or that an epidemic wiped out the villagers, the final survivor burying the corpses before moving on. A more plausible version of the legend suggests that the male population – all fishermen – were drowned at sea one stormy night, the women, over a period of time, simply going elsewhere in search of work. And, even more likely – if somewhat less romantic – is the theory that a move from their isolated fishing village was merely precipitated by a decline in fish stocks.

HUNGRY FOR ACTION

Farming is still a major industry in Cornwall and, like any industry, it has had its problems over the years.

The county was affected by the same potato blight that brought famine to Ireland. The Cornish potato famine of the 1840s meant that people had to look elsewhere for their staple food. This led to a large increase in the price of grain, also affected by poor harvests, and soon the average man could not afford to buy a loaf of bread.

Families were going hungry and there was much unrest. The rising price of food sparked riots and disturbances at a number of towns. The military had to intervene during the St Austell Bread Riots of 1847, when an angry mob brought terror to the high street, looting shops and demanding lower prices.

WE NEED TO TALK

Those living in remote areas are often last to benefit from the advances in telecommunications – now one of the biggest industries in the world.

And few would be that surprised to learn that some residents of Cornwall still complain of an inadequate internet connection.

So it is perhaps ironic that the very far corner of Cornwall – a sparsely populated area of a sparse county – was once the hub of global communications. Indeed, this incredible tale of enterprise and later espionage took place just a few miles from Land's End itself.

The beach at Porthcurno was the British termination point for a series of underwater telegraph cables that stretched to every corner of the world in the second half of the nineteenth century. Falmouth was initially chosen as the location for the cable station, but, being a busy port, there were fears that the cables had more chance of being damaged by passing ships. It meant remote Porthcurno, further west, got the nod, becoming home to the largest and busiest telegraph station in the world. Cables linked the UK with the British Empire. Messages from Porthcurno, sent via the cables, could reach their destinations within a minute.

However, on the other side of Mount's Bay at the beginning of the twentieth century, a rival had emerged. The famous Guglielmo Marconi was working on a wireless telegraphy system and set up a research centre at Poldhu, Mullion, on the Lizard peninsula. The Eastern Telegraph Company, in charge of the Porthcurno telegraph cable operation at the time, was not surprisingly unimpressed. Having virtually monopolised world communications since the 1870s, the firm feared for its future. It was still unclear whether Marconi was on to something big and so the Eastern Telegraph Company started to spy on the activities going on at Poldhu, setting up a secret listening post to monitor the base of its rival. Indeed, those at Porthcurno had good cause to worry. In 1901, signals sent from Poldhu were received by Marconi himself as far away as Newfoundland, a distance of some 2,000 miles. They were just three faint dots – Morse code for the letter 'S' – and even though much still needed to be done in the development of wireless technology, Marconi had showed the world that he could do it.

A lot has changed since that first transatlantic radio signal was successfully transmitted. Today, you can stand next to a monument on the cliffs at Poldhu that marks the spot where transatlantic wireless communications began. You might even wish to send a message via your own wireless device to Newfoundland or elsewhere in the world. And, as you do so, you might like to consider what went on at this remote spot in Cornwall to make that possible.

11

THE ARTS

LITERATURE, ART, ENTERTAINMENT AND SPORT

WORDS AND PICTURES

You cannot fail to be stirred by Cornwall; some would say it is the most inspirational county in England. So it is no surprise that its unique history, colourful people and diverse landscape have got the creative juices of writers and artists flowing over the years.

Novelist D.H. Lawrence wrote in 1916: 'Cornwall is very primeval: great, black, jutting cliffs and rocks, like the original darkness, and a pale sea breaking in, like dawn. It is like the beginning of the world, wonderful ...'

DAPHNE FOUND 'INN-SPIRATION' ON THE MOOR

Ask people to think of a Cornish writer and many will immediately think of Dame Daphne du Maurier. Of course, du Maurier was not Cornish. However, most of her novels were set in the county and it is fair to say that they did – and are still doing – more for tourism than many a glossy brochure has ever done.

Indeed, many will say that no other novels set in Cornwall quite captured the county as well as those from the pen of du Maurier. And, of course, in *Jamaica Inn*, she produced arguably the most famous Cornish novel of all time.

Du Maurier moved to Cornwall in the mid 1920s. She moved house on several occasions, but always remained in the Fowey area – her various homes appearing in different guises in novels such as *Rebecca* and *The House on the Strand*. Fellow author Sir Arthur Quiller-Couch – better known as 'Q' – lived in Fowey and du Maurier explored much of the county with his daughter, Foy.

It was 'Q' who persuaded du Maurier and Foy to go on a horse-riding trip to the real *Jamaica Inn*, at Bolventor, in 1930. At that time, it was actually a temperance house and a hospitable place, a far cry from the foreboding tavern depicted in the novel that du Maurier went on to write. However, Bodmin Moor is still a lonely place and the imagination of the author is said to have been stirred after the two ladies became lost in fog while out riding. Fortunately, their horses led them back to the inn. No damage was done and the seeds of one of the most famous books of the twentieth century were sown, *Jamaica Inn* eventually being published in 1936. The inn that inspired her classic tale of wrecking still stands just off the A30 and it is testament to the success of the book that the inn sign has perhaps become the most photographed in all England.

Du Maurier wrote great stories with great settings. No other 'foreigner' quite captured the essence of Cornwall in the same way. The author loved the county and respected it. She embraced its unique history, tradition and culture.

Her great understanding of Cornish history is particularly reflected in her novels, such as *The King's General*, set in the county during the English Civil War, but she also revealed her knowledge in non-fiction, such as in *Vanishing Cornwall*, where she herself admitted that she 'rambled on about the past'.

There is no doubt that du Maurier understood the spirit of Cornwall and its people. And, arguably, no one else has managed to capture it so successfully in fiction, which is why Daphne du Maurier – a 'foreigner' – can justifiably be claimed as probably Cornwall's greatest writer.

A TV 'WINNER'

It is difficult to believe that the successful *Poldark* novels were not penned by a Cornishman; author Winston Graham was born in Manchester.

However, like Daphne du Maurier, Graham lived and breathed Cornwall during his time in the county, filling his lungs with its spirit.

Thanks to two BBC adaptations of the *Poldark* books, many who have not even read a page of the twelve historical novels have been able to experience what life may have been like in the county at the end of the eighteenth and beginning of the nineteenth centuries. It is said that when the first *Poldark* series was on TV in the 1970s, some clergymen cancelled or moved their services as they were unable to compete with the programme. While fans of Aidan Turner – the actor who plays Ross Poldark in the latest television series – might disagree, the real star is the Cornish landscape itself. Windswept cliffs and secret coves are how many picture Cornwall. Graham, of course, used only words to draw his picture of a county so different from the others.

The author once said that he could have written the story of the Poldarks on the back of a postcard. However, it took a dozen novels in the end, spanning more than fifty years.

The first appeared in 1945 and the last in 2002, the year before his death.

Graham moved to Perranporth in 1925 at the age of 17. He stayed there for some thirty-five years. During that time, he immersed himself in the history of Cornwall, taking particular note of its mining industry, which played such an important part in the lives of so many. His novels successfully captured what was a significant era in the history of the county. And, in seasoning his stories with a little bit of romance, it is no surprise that the *Poldark* books of Graham continue to delight readers, offering them the very picture of Cornwall that they expect and want to see.

Of course, Cornwall always looks good on screen and the *Wycliffe* detective novels of Cornish-born writer W.J. Burley also transferred successfully from the page, the television series, starring Jack Shepherd, very popular in the 1990s.

HOME IS WHERE THE HEART IS

Poet Sir John Betjeman was among the 'foreigners' to make his home in Cornwall, and he, like Daphne du Maurier and Winston Graham, became almost an adopted Cornishman.

Certainly, Betjeman is so closely associated with Cornwall that some might argue that he is more Cornish than some Cornish-born authors!

Betjeman loved Cornwall and wrote much on the county – in verse and prose. His poems are much loved, but he also acquired a sound knowledge of the history and tradition of the duchy, penning a guide book as well.

The poet first tasted Cornwall on family holidays at Trebetherick, opposite Padstow. As an adult, he bought a house overlooking the golf course at St Enodoc, where he was laid to rest after his death, in the graveyard of the famous church that lies partly submerged in the dunes.

THEY FELL FOR CORNWALL

Writers have for many years been falling over themselves to experience the delights of Cornwall – in some cases ... literally.

Alfred, Lord Tennyson was perhaps the most famous holidaymaker. He came to Bude in 1848 in search of what he believed to be the highest waves in England. He was in so much of a hurry to see the sea, on arriving at what is now the Falcon Hotel, Tennyson ordered a maid to point him in the direction of the Atlantic Ocean. She obligingly opened the back door and pointed into the distance. Tennyson stumbled into the darkness and fell over a wall, dropping 6ft on to the beach, injuring his leg in the process and resulting in a six-week period of convalescence. He at least got to experience the warmth and generosity of the locals, with many willing to accommodate the famous visitor for free.

Tennyson wrote much about the north coast of Cornwall and its legends. It was at the castle in Tintagel – in the wind and rain – that he is said to have contemplated the story of King Arthur that later appeared in his famous poem *Idylls of the King*, which is – along with Sir Thomas Malory's fifteenth-century *Le Morte d'Arthur* – probably the most famous literary interpretation of the legend.

During his tour of the county, Tennyson visited the eccentric parson of Morwenstow, Robert Stephen Hawker, himself a man of words. Both literary men were full of admiration for the other and visited Tintagel together. At the end of the nineteenth century, the National Trust stepped in to preserve the area that so inspired Tennyson. The organisation bought the headland known as Barras Nose – its first coastal purchase – as a memorial to the poet and to prevent further development in the area.

Algernon Charles Swinburne was among the many to visit Tintagel. He came in the 1860s to finish *Atalanta in Calydon*, lodging with painter John William Inchbold. Swinburne, like Tennyson, also picked up an injury, cutting

Charles Dickens.

his foot while exploring nearby caves. And like Tennyson, Swinburne was drawn to the legends of Cornwall. *Tristram of Lyonesse* is one of many literary pieces inspired by the Tristan and Iseult story.

It was not just the legends of Cornwall – or big waves – that drew writers to its shores. Some came to broaden their minds, but others just came for a holiday.

Charles Dickens and Wilkie Collins were among the many Victorian writers to tour the duchy. The Spirit of Christmas Present in *A Christmas Carol* takes Scrooge to visit the family of a poor tin miner who lives on a 'bleak and desert moor, where monstrous masses of rude stone were cast about, as though it were the burial-place of giants'. Collins famously wrote about his visit to Botallack Mine, describing the descent in hellish terms, and leaving the reader in no doubt that the miners endured terrible working conditions.

R.M. Ballantyne stayed in West Penwith for a spell while researching the mining industry at St Just. The novel *Deep Down: A Tale of the Cornish Mines* resulted in 1868.

It is no wonder writers have been influenced by the Cornish landscape, whether it be the wild north or the pretty south.

Kenneth Grahame, author of *The Wind in the Willows*, started that book as a series of letters sent from the Greenbank Hotel, Falmouth, where he was staying in 1907. Grahame was particularly drawn to Fowey and got married in the town. There are many who claim he was thinking of Fowey when Rat describes 'the little grey sea town ... that clings along one steep side of the harbour'. Grahame became friends with Fowey author Sir Arthur Quiller-Couch and the two enjoyed 'messing about in boats'.

Virginia Woolf drew on early family holidays in St Ives for her novel *To the Lighthouse*. Her father, Sir Leslie Stephen, leased Talland House and that building and surrounding area left a lasting impression on the author. Although the book is set in the Inner Hebrides, it is really Cornwall and Godrevy Lighthouse that Woolf is describing.

Poet Laurence Binyon is said to have written *For the Fallen* while sitting on the cliffs at Pentire Point during a family holiday at Polzeath at the start of the First World War.

It was not the Cornish landscape that inspired Beatrix Potter – but a pig. She is said to have got the idea for *The Tale of Little Pig Robinson* when she saw a pig being loaded on to a ship at Falmouth. George Eliot is said to have been 'stranded' in Penzance for a week in 1857, the bad weather preventing her boat from making the trip to the Isles of Scilly. She used the time wisely, working on *Scenes of Clerical Life*.

George Bernard Shaw found the slower life of Cornwall beneficial and he began writing *The Doctor's Dilemma* with an 'intensity impossible in London'. He is said to have finished the first act on the beach and had completed the third at St Austell station while waiting for his train back to the capital.

A SOBERING THOUGHT
There are many different reasons why authors have come to Cornwall over the years. Many carried out research, some visited family or friends, while others just wanted to enjoy the view.

And Welsh poet Dylan Thomas did not just come on one occasion in 1936 to hang out – but to 'dry out'. Thomas always struggled with alcohol and hoped the change of scenery would help him overcome his addiction.

The poet already knew Cornwall well and ended up getting married in the duchy. He wed at Penzance in 1937, staying at Mousehole, which he described as the loveliest village in England. However, the choice of 'honeymoon' venue might not have been the greatest idea for one trying to beat the booze, the happy couple staying at the *Lobster Pot*, an inn. And a further move along the coast to Newlyn – where Thomas attended wild parties with the artists who frequented that town – probably would not have helped either!

LABOUR OF LOVE
Novelist Thomas Hardy fell in love with the charms of Cornwall – in more ways than one. It was not just the landscape that caught his eye, but one of the locals as well.

Hardy did not come to Cornwall for a holiday. He came because he was sent to the county for the purpose of work. However, this young architect from Dorchester who came to oversee the restoration of a north Cornwall church in 1870 was more than happy to return whenever he could.

The lady that won the heart of the young Hardy was Emma Gifford, the sister-in-law of the rector of St Juliot, near Boscastle. The writer got to know her during many visits to the church and she eventually was to become the first Mrs Hardy. Their love affair was the inspiration for Hardy's novel, *A Pair of Blue Eyes*, the most autobiographical of his works.

Cornwall and the home of Emma always remained in Hardy's heart, even after her death. He famously returned to this part of north Cornwall and poured out his grief in a number of poems, including *Beeny Cliff*, named after one of their many haunts. Hardy laments: 'The woman now is elsewhere, whom the ambling pony bore, and nor knows nor cares for Beeny, and will laugh there nevermore.'

EVERYBODY NEEDS GOOD NEIGHBOURS
Not all 'foreigners' who came to Cornwall were welcomed with open arms, and while most writers eulogised about their experiences in the duchy, D.H. Lawrence recounted his in the 'Nightmare' chapter of *Kangaroo*.

Lawrence did not intend for his Cornwall residency to turn out this way. He had hoped it would be his utopia, his aim being to set up an idealistic commune. The author first lived in Porthcothan, near Padstow, in 1915, staying at the home of fellow writer J.D. Beresford, and life there was good. After leaving Porthcothan, the Lawrences rented a cottage at Zennor. Lawrence was happy there at first as well.

The writers Katherine Mansfield and John Middleton Murry lived next door for a spell. However, the utopian ideal faded. After many arguments, Mansfield and Murry moved on. That was not the end of the problems for the Lawrences, however. Wife Frieda was related to the German war ace known as the Red Baron, and that fact alone made locals suspicious of their new neighbours. They believed they were spies and accused them of signalling to enemy submarines that were inflicting heavy losses on Allied ships in the area. The authorities did not trust the Lawrences either and, in 1917, the couple were forced to leave Zennor after police raided their home.

Lawrence did pen *Women in Love* in Cornwall and, if he had been allowed to stay, he might have gone on to produce some classic Cornish novels.

THE BAD GUY

Sometimes villains make for a better story than heroes. Polish–English author Joseph Conrad based the title character of *Lord Jim* on Porthleven seaman Augustine Podmore Williams. In 1880, Williams was first officer of the *Jeddah*, a ship taking almost a thousand Muslim pilgrims to Arabia. However, a fierce storm gave Williams great cause for concern. He persuaded the captain that they should abandon ship. Knowing that there were not enough lifeboats, they left the pilgrims to their fate. Williams and his fellow officers were rescued a few days later. The Cornish mariner and his accomplices spun a sorry tale: the ship had gone down with much loss of life, they informed the authorities. There was no reason for anyone not to believe them. However, it was not so. The ship had not met its doom and neither had the pilgrims. They were eventually rescued and the vessel was towed to Aden. Williams, in particular, was disgraced as a liar and coward at the subsequent inquiry. He spent the rest of his life as a water clerk in Singapore and – unlike Lord Jim who restores his honour – there is no evidence to say that Williams did likewise.

Conrad was himself a seaman before finding fame as a writer. It is believed he spent some nine months in Falmouth after his ship was forced to dock for repairs in the 1880s.

The biography of another European author – Rudolf Erich Raspe – contained a memorable villain as well … himself. The life of Raspe, who was described as a 'rogue' by his biographer, was almost as improbable as that of the title character of his most famous work, *The Surprising Adventures of Baron Munchausen*, a satirical fantasy that Raspe penned in Cornwall a century before Conrad had stayed in the county.

German-born Raspe perfected the book – later adapted as a film – while working as a chemist and copper smelter at Dolcoath Mine, Camborne. Despite his undoubted scientific knowledge, the eccentric Raspe was viewed as a crazy conjuror by many of the employees, performing tricks with flames and minerals. Raspe had escaped to England after being caught stealing treasures from the Kassel Museum when employed as a keeper of the collections of Frederick II.

LORD OF THE 'PRIZE'

So many writers are associated with Cornwall – many would find it difficult to pick out the Cornish ones.

And arguably the most famous scribe *born* in the duchy is someone who most would not necessarily associate with the county. That is because the multi-prizewinning Sir William Golding did not deliberately draw upon the history, landscape and people of Cornwall for his popular novels. While the likes of Daphne du Maurier and Winston Graham penned 'Cornish' stories, Golding chose not to focus on his native county when he picked up his pen. He just happened to be a writer who was a Cornishman, rather than a writer of Cornish things. Of course, that is still a good enough reason for the county to hail him as its greatest writer. Certainly, few have been so successful in terms of recognition and lasting fame. Many have grown up reading Golding's first and most famous novel, *Lord of the Flies*. Since publication in 1954, it has become a favourite in the classroom, often appearing on the school syllabus for English literature. The novel became an international bestseller and made Golding a household name. In the 1980s, *Rites of Passage* earned Golding the Booker Prize, and the author was later awarded the Nobel Prize in Literature.

Golding was born at St Columb Minor, near Newquay. Although he spent most of his life in other parts of the country, he did return 'home' in later life and died in Perranarworthal, near Falmouth.

Many Cornwall-born writers have made significant contributions to English literature. The county has produced many scribes, including D.M. Thomas, Jack Clemo and Charles Causley. A.L. Rowse was arguably the best known Cornishman throughout the world in the second half of the twentieth century, while the versatile Sir Arthur Quiller-Couch – better known as 'Q' – could make a similar claim for the first half.

Of course, some Cornish-born authors have almost been forgotten. Herman Cyril McNeile – aka Sapper – is a name few know, but his creation of Bulldog Drummond is familiar to many.

There is another now forgotten Cornishman who made an even bigger impact in the literary world, at least in terms of sales ...

THE FORGOTTEN BEST-SELLER
Novelist Silas Hocking probably regretted selling the copyright of his second book for just £20. That novel, *Her Benny*, went on to become the first book to sell a million copies during the lifetime of an author.

Her Benny did at least bring Hocking fame, if not a fortune. He became one of the most popular novelists of his day, no mean feat when you look at the competition. However, his fame has not lasted and while the novels of his Victorian contemporaries still fill bookshelves across the country, those of Hocking have largely been forgotten by the masses.

Hocking was born at St Stephen-in-Brannel, near St Austell, in 1850. He became a Methodist minister and this calling took him from the county to the north of England, which became the setting for *Her Benny*. The novel about the street urchins of Liverpool was published in 1879. Hocking's Methodism is apparent in many of his novels, most being didactic stories for children.

HE FOUND IT IN HIS 'ART'

One Cornish-based writer – as successful as any during his time – eventually became lost in the shadow of an individual he himself championed. However, his protégé was to make his mark not with a pen, but with a brush.

John Opie is known today as Cornwall's greatest painter. In contrast, satirist John Wolcot, who discovered him, is all but forgotten. And even if some do have some knowledge of Wolcot, it is probably through his association with Opie rather than through his own literary success.

Wolcot was also a medical man. He was practising as a physician in Truro when he discovered the teenage Opie, the son of a St Agnes carpenter. Wolcot recognised his talent and bought him out of his carpentry apprenticeship, Opie's father less than keen for his son to pursue a career in art. Wolcot bought Opie all the materials he needed and provided him with a studio at his Truro home. Eventually both writer and artist headed for London, where Wolcot became the most popular satirist of the late eighteenth century, writing under the name Peter Pindar, and Opie became the most famous portrait painter of the time. Members of the royal family, and other notable men and women, were among Opie's subjects.

Wolcot marketed Opie as the 'Cornish Wonder'. He introduced the country boy to fashionable society and, crucially, to the great and influential Sir Joshua Reynolds. Opie has often been labelled the 'English Rembrandt', his most famous painting being *The Murder of Rizzio*.

Wolcot also helped launch the career of another Truro artist. Henry Bone, who became arguably the greatest enamel painter of all time, was discovered painting designs on porcelain buttons and brooches while working for china clay manufacturer William Cookworthy. Wolcot used his influence to help Bone prosper when the latter moved to London. Bone went on to become the official royal enamellist to various monarchs, his son Henry Pierce inheriting his talent and following in his footsteps.

Thomas Luny was another Cornish-born painter to enjoy much success. Like Opie he left Cornwall at a young age, also becoming famous at the end of the eighteenth century. Luny is believed to have been born at St Ewe, near Mevagissey. He never lost his love of the sea and it became the inspiration for his works.

A 'PORT' OF PAINT

As Cornish-born artists John Opie, Henry Bone and Thomas Luny were leaving the county to further their careers – other painters were arriving.

Indeed, it was not only writers who came to Cornwall for inspiration. Artists have been doing so for centuries as well. Painters J.M.W. Turner and John William Inchbold both famously captured the dramatic landscape of Tintagel, among other things.

However, towards the end of the nineteenth century, many of the leading British painters had settled in France and had to 'rediscover' the duchy. After training on the Continent, particularly in fashionable Paris, a considerable number moved to Brittany to benefit from the long hours of daylight offered in the west. But sometimes you can travel far for something, only to discover that it is also available a little closer to home. And that is why the fishing port of Newlyn became the unlikely home of British art from the 1880s.

Artists came to realise that Newlyn offered the same attractions as Brittany. Members of the Newlyn School – the name given to the colony of painters that worked in and around the town – were drawn by the low cost of living on the Celtic peninsula, as well as the long hours of daylight. Its remote position meant that Newlyn, like Brittany, had not been scarred by the Industrial Revolution. Those who came to Newlyn found the people were going about their lives just like their ancestors had done. Little had changed and the artists found inspiration in this, often painting local fishermen and capturing everyday life in and around the harbour.

One of the first artists to make his home in Newlyn was Walter Langley, who moved to the town in 1882. By the end of 1884, the Newlyn School consisted of almost thirty painters.

One of those charmed by Newlyn was Stanhope Forbes. He too came from France, but struggled to explain why he and his fellow painters should have chosen Newlyn in particular. He wrote:

> What lodestone of artistic metal the place [Newlyn] contains I know not, but its effects were strongly felt in the studios of Paris and Antwerp particularly, by a number of young English painters studying there, who just about then, by some common impulse, seemed drawn towards this corner of their native land.

Forbes and his wife founded an official school of art in 1899, which brought a new wave of artists to the area. Some went on to settle further along the coast at Lamorna, creating almost a splinter group that is sometimes referred to as the later Newlyn School.

The Newlyn School, as a movement, only lasted into the early twentieth century, but Newlyn still has a thriving art colony today.

Nearby St Ives, on the north coast, is, of course, also famous for art. James Whistler and Walter Sickert were both captivated by the town and surrounding area.

And it was not just painters who found inspiration here. Bernard Leach and Shoji Hamada set up a pottery in the town in 1920. And, at the outbreak of the Second World War, sculptor Dame Barbara Hepworth moved to St Ives with husband Ben Nicholson, who was a particular admirer of primitive painter Alfred Wallis, a resident of St Ives and, notably, Cornish by birth, unlike most who were drawn to the area. Wallis painted on anything he could find: driftwood, cardboard and even his cottage walls.

Enticed by the famed special quality of light found at St Ives, a new wave of painters followed after the war and today, like Newlyn, the seaside resort is famous for art, helped, of course, by the opening of Tate St Ives in 1980, the gallery built partly on the site of the studio and garden once belonging to Barbara Hepworth.

Cornwall did, of course, produce a famous sculptor of its own in the previous century. However, Neville Northey Burnard, who was born at Altarnun on the edge of Bodmin Moor, wasted his talent and died a pauper. At his prime, many leading lights of fashionable London became his subjects, including Charles Dickens. Burnard was responsible for the statue of explorer Richard Lander that stands in Truro.

NOW FOR A DIFFERENT TUNE

Music – like art and literature – also forms an important part of Cornish culture, so it is not surprising that many born in Cornwall have gone on to great things.

Two of the finest voices developed in the duchy enriched both ends of the nineteenth century.

George III called St Keverne-born Charles Incledon the 'British national singer'. Incledon was the leading operatic tenor of his day, bringing music to the ears of London audiences at the end of the eighteenth and beginning of the nineteenth centuries.

For the ladies, Redruth-born Fanny Moody had few equals at the end of the nineteenth century. One of her contemporaries was the famous Dame Nellie Melba, but, at the time, Fanny – known as the 'Cornish Nightingale' – was as much loved.

Cornish composer Thomas Merritt also enjoyed much success at the time. He wrote music for all occasions, including a march for the coronation of Edward VII in 1902. Illogan-born Merritt is also remembered for his Christmas carols.

On the stage, Cornwall also produced a leading lady. Launceston-born Mary Ann Davenport became, according to many, the greatest character actress London has ever known. If Samuel Foote – who delighted audiences in the eighteenth century – was the most famous Cornish actor, Mary was at the top of the tree among the women. She was leading lady at Convent Garden from about 1794 to 1830, thought to be longer than any other actor or actress.

Cornwall itself has also been the inspiration for many in the theatre and one Cornish town, in particular, has been immortalised through arguably the most famous operetta of all time. *The Pirates of Penzance*, the work of Gilbert and Sullivan, was first performed in 1879.

DON'T MAKE SPORT OF US

Cornwall is not exactly a hotbed of sport. It still has no club in the Football League and the county is yet to grace the top flight of cricket.

It is on the rugby field where it has enjoyed most success, trips to Twickenham now a regular occurrence for followers of the county game.

Individually, Cornishmen and women have also made their mark and many happily sit among the sporting greats.

BIG HIT AT THE 'BOX' OFFICE
There are many 'superstars' in sport these days. Indeed, the label has perhaps been too liberally attached to some sportsmen and sportswomen.

However, there is no argument that Cornish boxer Bob Fitzsimmons is deserving of the title, to go with the many that he won in the ring. In fact, it is perhaps fair to say that Fitzsimmons was one of the first superstars of sport. He certainly played his part in making sport what it is today.

As a boxer, Fitzsimmons achieved much greatness at the end of the nineteenth and beginning of the twentieth centuries. He was Britain's first world heavyweight champion and went on to win world titles at three different weights, the first man to do so. However, it was his personality and charisma that really made him a superstar. The public could not get enough of him. Because there was no television or even radio when he beat Jim Corbett to become world heavyweight champion in 1897, it is said that some 50,000 people gathered in City Hall Park, New York, just to hear the result. That was indicative of the draw Fitzsimmons had on people. He was a larger-than-life character who became just as famous for his exploits outside of the ring. He dined with presidents and trained for his fights by wrestling a lion, one of many exotic animals he kept as pets. Married several times, Fitzsimmons lived life to the full and became famous all over the world.

Helston – the birthplace of Fitzsimmons – was not home for long. He was still a boy when he moved to New Zealand. His fighting career started there and continued in Australia, but it only really took off after he had moved to the United States. It was his world middleweight championship win over Jack Dempsey in 1891 that made the world sit up and take notice, Dempsey being hot favourite and Fitzsimmons largely unknown at the time.

For the next five years, Fitzsimmons remained unbeaten. And then, when he did finally lose to Tom Sharkey, many are of the belief that he was unfairly denied victory by none less than famous gunslinger Wyatt Earp, whose fondness for upholding the law also took him into boxing rings as a referee on occasions. However, some questioned whether he became a law unto himself. On this occasion, he entered the ring with his legendary Colt 45 still in his holster and had to be reminded to remove it. It might have been wise to check his pockets too, as many were of the belief that Earp had been slipped a bundle of money before the fight to ensure that Sharkey triumphed. Fitzsimmons floored Sharkey, but Earp disqualified him on a technicality.

The defeat of Corbett in what was labelled 'the fight of the century' was the one that really earned Fitzsimmons a place in boxing history, that event being the first championship bout ever filmed. It was held in Carson City – mining country. A large number of Cornish emigrant miners were present to cheer on one of their own. The win over Corbett was remarkable because Fitzsimmons was a natural middleweight, but it proved that he could still beat men several stone heavier.

Although Fitzsimmons eventually lost his heavyweight title, he did, aged 41, become light heavyweight champion, becoming the first boxer to win world titles at three different weights.

Fitzsimmons revelled in his status as a celebrity. Because he was so prominent outside the ring – mixing with high society – he helped change the image of the sport, giving it respectability following its early days of unregulated bare-knuckle brawls.

They say sport has no personalities these days and they are probably right if you compare them to Bob Fitzsimmons, arguably Cornwall's greatest sporting superstar.

ALL ABOUT WINGS

Rugby has always had a place in the hearts of the Cornish, and yet the county's greatest rugby player preferred ... pigeons.

While the likes of Cornish boxer Bob Fitzsimmons could not get enough of the limelight, wing Bert Solomon did his best to shun it.

On the day Solomon was due to win his first cap for the England rugby team in 1910, excited fans packed the

station at Redruth to see him off to Twickenham. However, when the train pulled in, Solomon was nowhere to be seen. A search party was sent to his house and there Solomon was found with his pigeons. It is said that a number had not returned home and he was reluctant to set off until they had done so, even if that meant giving up his international debut. His fans had to escort him to the station, where the rest of the supporters had persuaded the guard not to let the train go without their local hero.

Solomon eventually got to Twickenham and played a starring role in the victory over Wales, but that was enough for him. He did not want to repeat the experience and quit the international game after winning that one cap. It appears that Solomon did not enjoy the social life that went with the sport of rugby – he genuinely preferred to be with his pigeons.

Cornwall has produced some fine rugby players over the years, but Solomon must have been very special. He had only played a couple of times for the first team at Redruth when he was selected to represent his county. At the beginning of the twentieth century, county rugby was big. Many believed it to be more of an honour to represent Cornwall than England. Of course, even today, many claim to be Cornish first and English second! In 1908, county champions Cornwall represented Britain at the Olympic Games in London, Solomon among those to pick up a silver medal following defeat to Australia in the final.

Solomon would probably have gone on to even greater things if his heart had really been in the sport. As well as turning down further opportunities to play for his country, it is said he also declined a very lucrative offer to become a rugby league player. His fans were not the only ones who had to go that extra mile to ensure he took to the field. On match days, his club would arrange for a horse and carriage to turn up at his house to take him to the game. Many rugby fans would only go to matches to watch Solomon and, it is said, his very appearance would put an extra 1,000 through the turnstiles.

IN 'OAR' OF ANN

Gig racing may not be the most popular sport outside of Cornwall these days, but towards the middle of the nineteenth century, few in England had not heard of Ann Glanville. She was dubbed champion female rower of the world by the press and became a household name.

Glanville, who was born at Saltash in 1796, rowed virtually all her long life. She had no need to train for competitions as her husband was a waterman and she would assist him in ferrying passengers across the River Tamar.

Big and strong, Glanville was not only better than any other female rower in Cornwall, but also most of the men.

She skippered an all-women crew that regularly beat male opponents at regattas throughout the country. There are stories of an impressed Queen Victoria being present on one such occasion – the monarch supposedly joining the rest of the crowd in cheering the Saltash ladies to victory.

Ann Glanville – despite giving birth to no fewer than fourteen children – continued competitive rowing until she was in her sixties.

THE 'NATIONAL' SPORT OF CORNWALL

There is, of course, one sport that Cornwall is synonymous with – surfing. Fistral Beach, Newquay, is now considered to be the surfing centre of the UK.

If surfing became the principal pastime in Cornwall in the twentieth century, wrestling held that honour in the nineteenth. Thousands once attended wrestling matches and there was serious money to be had for those involved. The most famous Cornish wrestler of the era was James Polkinghorne. His meetings against Devon champion Abraham Cann in the 1820s were much anticipated.

Wrestling has always been popular in Cornwall and was probably its 'national' sport as far back as at least the fifteenth century, when Cornishmen going into battle at Agincourt in 1415 displayed an image of two wrestlers in a hitch on their banner of war.

If wrestling was not the 'national' sport of Cornwall, Cornish hurling probably was. And it appears the game could be as rough as any, parish records revealing that a player was killed during a contest at Camborne in 1705.

OFF THE BEATEN TRACK

Cornwall is perhaps the last place in England where you would expect to hear the roar of Formula One motor racing cars, but that was the case in the 1950s. Three Formula One race meetings were held at Davidstow, near Camelford, between 1954 and 1955.

Many redundant airfields throughout the country were transformed into racing circuits following the Second World War. Davidstow only enjoyed a brief moment in the sun, and that is perhaps a fitting description, as poor weather conditions – the circuit being situated on the fringes of Bodmin Moor – contributed to its demise.

One Cornishman to make his mark in motor sport was Donald Healey. Not only did he race cars – he also designed and built them, the Austin-Healey becoming one of the most famous sports cars of the twentieth century. As a driver, Healey, who was born at Perranporth, had many successes, including winning the famous Monte Carlo Rally in 1931.

12

MODERN MISCELLANY

FROM WAR TO EDEN

MIND YOUR LANGUAGE

The start of the twentieth century was a significant one for Cornwall. The man labelled as the 'Father of the Cornish Revival' was Henry Jenner; he reinforced the Celtic identity of the county. Through his work, people were inspired to preserve – and revitalise – Cornish culture and traditions. And some went as far as even learning the language. To assist them, Jenner published *A Handbook of the Cornish Language* in 1904. In the same year, he also successfully campaigned for Cornwall to join the Celtic Congress. Membership of this international organisation meant that Cornwall was now recognised as a Celtic nation.

In 1920, Jenner became president of the first Old Cornwall Society, set up in St Ives. Four years later he was made overall president of all of those societies, their aim being to preserve the culture and traditions of the county.

With fellow Cornish revivalist Robert Morton Nance, Jenner went on to form the Gorsedh Kernow, becoming its first Grand Bard. The first Gorsedh ceremony took place at

Boscawen-Un – the Bronze Age stone circle near St Buryan – in 1928.

The ideas of Jenner and Nance – who wrote a Cornish dictionary – were encapsulated in the formation of Mebyon Kernow (Sons of Cornwall) in 1951. Formed as a pressure group, it became a political party believing in the right of self-government in Cornwall. It is still fighting for Cornish nationalism today.

It was not until the start of the twenty-first century that the UK government officially recognised Cornish as a language, but the fact that people are even learning it today is a lasting tribute to the likes of Jenner. At the start of the twentieth century, the language was all but dead, many claiming it died at the death of the 'last' native speaker of Cornish, Dolly Pentreath, in 1777.

But Jenner never believed it ever died. He wrote: 'There has never been a time when there has been no person in Cornwall without a knowledge of the Cornish language.'

PRIDE OF THE CITY
It was not until 1910 that Truro Cathedral was finally completed after taking thirty years.

Queen Victoria granted Truro city status in 1877, just after the re-establishment of Cornwall as a diocese, Truro chosen as the see following hundreds of years of ecclesiastical control at Exeter in what was a joint diocese with Devon.

Edward White Benson, the first bishop of Truro, believed the Church of England needed a 'citadel' in Cornwall for its 'fight' against the Methodists, that movement still flourishing.

Work started in 1880 – the cathedral being built on the site of the parish church of St Mary. The cathedral was consecrated in 1887, but due to lack of finances, was not finally completed until the opening of two towers in 1910.

Today, Truro remains the only city in Cornwall. It has not always been the county town, however. Launceston,

Lostwithiel and Bodmin all held the seat of government at various times.

ONE DAY I'LL FLY AWAY

Richard Pearse – the son of a Cornwall emigrant – was a man flying high at the start of the twentieth century. And there are claims that it was he – and not the Wright brothers – who was the first to build and successfully fly an airplane.

Pearse possibly took to the skies in New Zealand in 1903, many months before the Wrights. However, evidence to support the theory is contradictory and inconclusive, meaning that most outside Pearse's native New Zealand have no idea of his pioneering feats in aviation.

Digory Pearse, Richard's father, was a native of South Petherwin and educated at Launceston before moving to New Zealand. He had lived in Cornwall at a time when the duchy was, of course, renowned for its engineers and inventors.

A WAR OF WORDS

'We will remember them.' So wrote poet Laurence Binyon in reference to the many who lost their lives during the early skirmishes of the First World War.

Many Cornishmen were killed on foreign soil. Fishermen, already well accustomed to life at sea, were called up as naval reservists. Needless to say, a great number did not return home. In fact, entire communities were destroyed in the Great War. The farming hamlet of Hille, near Looe, was a victim. It is said that not one of its men returned home from the fighting and its dwellings were eventually abandoned.

Binyon's poem, *For the Fallen*, is quoted at Remembrance Sunday services all over the country today. He penned it on the cliffs of north Cornwall in September 1914.

There was plenty of German submarine activity off the Cornish coast during the war, as another writer – D.H. Lawrence – was only too aware, he being accused of

secretly signalling to the enemy while residing at Zennor.
A major airship station – RNAS Mullion – was set up on
The Lizard to keep the German U-boats at bay.

Cornish ports, including Penzance and Falmouth, not
surprisingly played key roles, becoming temporary naval
bases. However, on the whole, the role Cornwall played
during the 'war to end all wars' was not as big as the one it
was to assume in the war to follow.

IN THE WARS AGAIN

The threat to Cornwall during the Second World War did not only come by way of the sea, but also the air.

Plymouth took many of the Luftwaffe hits in the south-west, but the duchy suffered as well. Perhaps unsurprisingly, Mount Edgcumbe House, overlooking Plymouth Sound, on the Cornish side of the Tamar, was hit during the Blitz of 1941. Looe Island was also bombed during the war; it is believed the German airmen mistook it for a British warship.

Not even Menabilly – the former home of Dame Daphne du Maurier – was considered sacred. Floodlights were positioned around a lake on the estate to fool the enemy into thinking it was the port of nearby Fowey.

Ports and harbours were obvious targets. Penzance and Penryn were both bombed on a number of occasions. The former suffered greatly and it is estimated that more than 800 bombs were dropped on the town and surrounding area.

Falmouth, with one of the largest natural harbours in the world, became home to so many British and Allied ships that at one point it was reported that you could walk across the estuary by stepping from one boat to the next.

Castles built by the likes of Henry VIII to keep out potential invaders hundreds of years ago were strengthened, now ready to keep a new enemy at bay. Pendennis Castle became the command centre for Cornwall, co-ordinating the protection of not only the port of Falmouth and its coastline, but also the western approaches of Britain itself. New coastal defences were also added, many pillboxes still littering the Cornish cliffs.

The threat from the sea, as well as the air, was also still very real. A number of British and Allied vessels were torpedoed in Cornish waters, including HMS *Warwick*, which went down off Trevose Head on the north coast in 1944 with the loss of many lives.

A number of RAF airfields and radar stations were established in Cornwall, though, of course, it was not all about defence. Many offensives had their roots in the county. Soldiers, tanks and equipment left Cornish soil bound for the beaches of Normandy.

Even the quiet Roseland peninsula became an assembly point for American troops, and General Eisenhower famously stayed at Tolverne Cottage on the banks of the River Fal in the run-up to the D-Day landings.

Some Cornish soldiers paid the ultimate price in Normandy. Because so many lost their lives in the Battle for Hill 112 – an important area of high ground near Caen – the French renamed it 'Cornwall Hill'.

However, compared to other counties, Cornwall, on the whole, perhaps got off lightly during the Second World War. Indeed, it is said that the British government privately conceded that if the country had been invaded – as Hitler planned to do – Cornwall would probably have been abandoned to the Germans.

OIL AND WATER

Cornwall is used to shipwrecks; however, one wreck off its coast in the twentieth century gained more publicity than any other.

The *Torrey Canyon* oil spill disaster of 1967 hit the headlines all over the world. The tanker – one of the world's biggest at the time – was carrying about 120,000 tonnes of crude oil when it ran aground between Land's End and the Isles of Scilly, at Seven Stones Reef. Britain had not witnessed anything like it before. In fact, the world had not seen an oil slick so big. Within just a few days, it was 35 miles by 25 miles in size. It was estimated that some 200,000 birds became contaminated. Many are of the belief that the environmental disaster was made worse by the use of detergent to try to disperse the slick, while the RAF and Royal Navy were derided for their attempts to bomb the stricken tanker in a bid to sink it. In the end, only favourable weather – and time – finally did the trick. The incident remains Britain's worst oil spill.

WEATHER THE STORM

Not all disasters have been the fault of man. There is little he can do to control the weather. Cornwall, like most counties, has endured many a storm over the centuries.

However, one incident within living memory sits among the worst of them, even though, incredibly, there was no loss of life. The Boscastle flood of 2004 put that north-coast fishing port on the map, even though it was not the only place in the area to be affected, nearby Crackington Haven, among the others.

However, all eyes outside of the duchy were solely on Boscastle at the time. Television viewers all over the world watched remarkable pictures of cars, boats and buildings being swept out to sea following the flash floods. People clinging to roofs and trees had to be rescued by helicopters, while dozens of houses were destroyed.

STILL LEADING THE WAY

Despite its pioneering achievements in industry during the Industrial Revolution and in the years that followed, many still see Cornwall as a backwater of England. However, the duchy has led the way on many fronts during the twentieth century as well.

In 1962, Britain's first satellite Earth station was established at Goonhilly Downs on the Lizard peninsula – it also being at the time the largest satellite station in the world. It was to play a major role in the first transatlantic TV transmission, and several years later went on to beam pictures of the moon landings to viewers.

Cornwall was the first county in England to introduce a dedicated helicopter emergency service, its air ambulance established in 1987. And Cornwall became a leader in renewable energy in 1991, the first commercial onshore wind farm in Britain established at Delabole, near Camelford.

Into the twenty-first century, Cornwall was still at it, creating a tourist attraction like no other. The Eden Project, near St Austell, which opened in 2001, is reputedly home to the largest greenhouse in the world. It attracts thousands of visitors every year and has made Cornwall known to even more people in every 'corner' of the globe.

INDEX